The
SACRED
LANGUAGE
of
TREES

The
SACRED
LANGUAGE
of
TREES

A.T. Mann

STERLING ETHOS
New York

STERLING ETHOS
New York

An Imprint of Sterling Publishing
387 Park Avenue South
New York, NY 10016

© 2012 by A. T. Mann
Interior design by Michele Trombley

ISBN 978-1-4027-6731-9

Distributed in Canada by Sterling Publishing
c/o Canadian Manda Group, 165 Dufferin Street
Toronto, Ontario, Canada M6K 3H6
Distributed in the United Kingdom by GMC Distribution Services
Castle Place, 166 High Street, Lewes, East Sussex, England BN7 1XU
Distributed in Australia by Capricorn Link (Australia) Pty. Ltd.
P.O. Box 704, Windsor, NSW 2756, Australia

For information about custom editions, special sales,
and premium and corporate purchases, please contact Sterling Special Sales
at 800-805-5489 or specialsales@sterlingpublishing.com.

Manufactured in the United States of America

2 4 6 8 10 9 7 5 3 1

www.sterlingpublishing.com

Produced by Authorscape Inc.

Dedication

To the sacred blessing we receive from the trees.

⌒

Acknowledgments

I would like to thank my many friends who helped and supported me throughout the writing and editing of this book. Thanks especially to Franziska Beveridge, who carefully read the text after completion and provided many very helpful insights and comments throughout. I also thank Judith Wheelock, whose support was positive and consistent, as always, and for her tree photograph. I also thank Barbara Berger and Kate Zimmermann of Sterling for their continuous support, careful editing, and help through the process. I also thank Martin Brading for generously allowing me to use his photographs of Indian sacred trees. I also thank the Woodstock Druid, who supported my inspiration to enter the sacred realm of the trees.

CONTENTS

24 November 1975   OAGvo   London

✤ Prologue—A Dream ✤

A WOMAN WALKS LABORIOUSLY ON BEACH stones along the base of a cliff, hemmed in by the sea's crashing breakers. Walking along the bottom of a gnarled cliff face, she looks up and sees the roots of a gigantic tree towering overhead. Weathered stones that have been ground down by the powerful sea surround her, making it difficult to walk, but she trudges ahead with labored steps. The tree's roots are open to view along the cliff face, snaking around in an almost Celtic pattern, like woven hair or ancient runes, narrowing more and more as they reach sea level. She can almost detect signs and sigils in the morass. As she follows the root structure down toward where she stands, all the massive roots acquiesce, and collect into a single strand meandering down to the bottom of the hill. This arboreal thread passes into the top of a cave, into which she crawls, following the roots to their source.

Entering the darkness on her hands and knees, she sees a glimmer of light ahead and notices that the root structure of this tree of life emanates from a single, rosy red apple that rests on a white marble column at the center of the cave. It radiates an ethereal light that

A. T. Mann, *Apple Tree Dream*, 1975

bathes the entire space. The light lends the cave interior an almost supernatural glow that contrasts eerily with the darkness and gloom; it seems to signify hope—almost a resurrection into another level of being. She is amazed by the primal nature and energy of this place and deeply feels its sanctity.

She touches the roots with her hands and feels their vibrancy, as though she is communing with the essence of the tree, if not of life itself. She can sense profound and complex activity at the core of its life, though it beats with a barely perceptible and leisurely rhythm. Despite the roughness of the bark, her hands melt into the texture of this shrine of nature. A gentle energy pulsates where the root penetrates the apple, just barely existing at the boundary of her awareness. The apple is a seed that provides nutrition for this huge tree, and perhaps for the entire world.

The woman returns to the outside, crawling and then stooping as she moves through the narrow passageway into the light. Outside, as she looks up at the tree perched at the crown of the hill, she sees that the sun is now shining through the treetop. A solitary ray pierces the branches and shines down onto her upraised face, as though directed into her searching eyes. She feels the intensity of this illumination, which momentarily blinds her . . . and she closes her eyes.

Michele Trombley, *Tree*

PLAS LLANDECWYN   29 SEPTEMBER 1974

THE LANGUAGE
OF THE SACRED TREES

The groves were God's first temples.
—WILLIAM CULLEN BRYANT, "A FOREST HYMN" (1860)

WHEN I WAS A YOUNG boy, trees seemed to me the oldest beings on the planet and a source of great unspoken wisdom. I loved the nooks and crannies of the roots as they wound into the earth, sometimes surfacing in various directions that bespoke their depth and solidity. My father had died during the war, just before I was born, and the trees seemed a kind of deeper and more immediate family to me, compensating for my primal loss.

In the early 1970s, I moved to England with my infant daughter and soon acquainted myself with an amazing group of people who had talent and great interest in music, the visual arts, theater, writing,

A. T. Mann, *Oak at Plas Llandecwyn*, 1974

Jungian psychology, symbolism, and the traditional high bohemian culture of Europe. On weekends, and for weeks at a stretch during the summer months, we would travel to North Wales where my dear friend, the brilliant musician and Jungian Peter Hartman, lived. The house, called Plas Llandecwyn, stood near Harlech Castle—built in 1283 BCE, probably on the site of an earlier sixth-century fortress—and within view of Mount Snowdon, where the ancient Druids performed their initiations. Plas was also close to the strange peninsular village of Portmerion, near Penrhyndeudraeth, where the 1960s television series *The Prisoner* was filmed.[1]

All around this magical countryside were old trees distorted by the constant winds and rain. Small, solitary stones jutted out of the ground in fields full of sheep. Long, centuries-old stone walls sparkled with tiny quartz crystals as they snaked across the countryside. Puncturing the landscape were deep valleys with strange, miniaturized vegetation and quarries where slate was mined, with waste mountains of stone fragments nearby.

Plas itself had walls that were four feet thick and made of stacked stone and slate, which protected the voluminous interior from the howling winter winds that blasted across the hillsides. Dominating the main entrance hall was a huge octagonal piece of slate. My theory is that the house was originally built as a chapel during medieval times and later became the residence of a minor lord. Whatever its origins, it carried a magnetic presence that you could feel throughout the house. Using a conical crystal pendulum suspended from pure white silk thread, I detected a variety of inviting places whose energies were palpable.

One day I held my pendulum over the octagonal stone in the hall, and it immediately began an odd series of movements. The pendulum swung back and forth several times in a particular direction, and then it rotated 60 degrees in a clockwise direction and started swinging again in a straight line. It repeated this unusual movement until completing the circle. I plotted the exact directions with a compass on a diagram of the house, and after a while I realized that the pendulum might be pointing at something outside of the house. I went out to investigate; what I found was extraordinary.

Each of the angles pointed toward the various trees that surrounded the house. What is more, all of the trees were a part of the ancient Celtic tree language. There were oak, willow, ash, hawthorn, holly, and hazel trees at various distances from the house, forming a magical circle that ostensibly protected and sanctified the place from its earliest days. This discovery brought such a feeling of sheer bliss that I remember it vividly today.

At that time I was just learning about what Robert Graves called the Beth-Luis-Nion Celtic Tree Alphabet for a chapter in the *Phenomenon Book of Calendars*, which we were writing and creating. Graves identified this tree alphabet as having been used in the Celtic countries, and especially in North Wales. In the process, I discovered that networks of sacred trees, likely planted by Druid priests, stretched

....

WITH NINE SORTS OF FACULTY
GOD HAD GIFTED ME:
I AM THE FRUIT OF FRUITS GATHERED
FROM NINE SORTS OF TREE.
—*Book of Taliesin*, "The Battle of the Trees"
(c. fourteenth century CE)[1]

over that part of North Wales. My friends and I recreated various calendar systems, including the lunar calendars of Islam and Judaism, the astrological calendars of the Chinese and Hindus, and early calendars derived from natural rhythms of the Aztec, Inca, and Polynesians. We also published a planting calendar, which integrated astrological phases and moon signs that are beneficial for planting, harvesting, and storing grains.

Trees are so powerful and inherent in our lives that when we come to such revelations—that they are not inanimate objects but rather profound life forms that bless our world—we align ourselves firmly with nature and begin to commune with the wisdom of the natural world.

The ecological crisis brings the indispensability of trees home on many levels. By converting carbon dioxide into oxygen, trees are the

Ancient Willow-Person of Braemer, England

natural living beings that compensate most for global warming, so it is essential that we retain as many of them as possible in all parts of the globe. Furthermore, while trees store carbon dioxide throughout their lifetimes, when they are cut down they release a great deal more carbon dioxide into the atmosphere than if they die and decompose naturally. It is therefore crucial to halt the practice of wide-scale deforestation.

In ancient times, the deep forests that covered most continents were sources of mystery, sites of myth, and places where strange beings and unknown dangers lurked. Nowadays, parents are reluctant to allow youngsters to go play in the woods, even if they appear safe. The fact that forests all over the world, including in North America, are continuing to disappear at a staggering rate eliminates these forested sanctuaries from our culture not only physically, but also psychologically. That, added to the clear-cutting of almost all North American forests in the last two hundred years, means that the threats of the wild woods virtually do not exist today. Indeed, in his book *Last Child in the Woods: Saving Our Children from Nature-Deficit Disorder* (2009), Richard Louv examines how, unlike previous generations of young children, the last few generations of American kids have grown up without really exploring and interacting with nature on their own. The causes of this reluctance to explore include addiction to electronics, a fear of being alone, a fear of being out of electronic touch, and their parents' fear of potential abductions—all of which are serious issues in our modern society. Louv believes that this profound lack of experience with and awareness of the natural world affects not only the physical and emotional health of the young, but also spells disaster for the future of the environmental movement.[2] However, by rediscovering the inner mysteries of trees, we might again find a place for them in our outer world today.

In his 1995 book *Landscape and Memory*, historian Simon Schama describes the layers of meaning that exist in apparently common landscapes and architecture around us:

> Beneath the commonplace is a long, rich, and significant history of associations between the pagan primitive grove and its tree idolatry, and the distinctive forms of Gothic architecture. ... In fact it goes directly to the heart of one of our most powerful yearnings: the craving to find in nature a consolation for our mortality.[2]

Schama realizes that we are drawn to nature to find satisfaction for mysteries with which we have lost touch—we intuitively seek the solace of groves of trees. Spending more time in the woods would further our awareness of the natural yearly cycles that trees show us, perhaps more than any other element in our landscape. As he implies, trees are an essential part of our interior landscape as well.

We know that we must save the trees on our planet for a number of logical reasons. One is to ensure that we have adequate oxygen. Another is to stabilize the basic integrity of the soil in order to retain and purify diminishing supplies of ground water. A third reason for eliminating the clear-cutting of vast expanses of jungle and forests around the globe is to preserve the delicate ecosystems that sustain the thousands of living species on which we all depend in one way or another. Trees also provide the wood from which paper pulp is created. Without giving thought to how we can conserve this valuable resource, how would we be able to enjoy the myriad of beautiful printed books such as this one? Together with our disconnection from the world of nature symbolized by the trees and their forests, it is very important that we resuscitate many of the myths, stories, and legends about trees from former cultures, not because we realistically advocate returning to the ways of those "noble savages" of ancient times. Rather, in order to restore the health of our environment, we must rediscover the sanctity of trees, discover how to revere them again, and learn how central they are to our relationships to nature and between each other. Part of this process is to re-enchant the world of nature, to learn to understand its language.

We can glean a vast quantity of information about the natural world through the prism of ancient culture: creation myths, religious worldviews, poetry, folk tales, and art enable us to see and understand the relationship between human beings and their surroundings in a different light. When we begin to understand this dynamic, we open ourselves to the possibility of reactivating a lost sensitivity through the vast knowledge that trees possess and are able to communicate to us. By simply running our hand over finely crafted wooden furniture, holding a great tree in our embrace, or even taking natural remedies that come from the trees, we begin to feel again how important they are for our very being.

The first temples were trees that were ceremonially decorated with symbols of the gods. Early temple architecture reflected the glory of these simple places by abstracting the elements of the natural world in architecture. As English architect and historian William Lethaby stated in his 1892 book, *Architecture, Mysticism, and Myth*:

> When the world was a tree, every tree was in some sort its representation; when a tent or a building, every tent or building; but when the relation was firmly established, there was action and reaction between the symbol and the reality, and ideas taken from one were transferred to the other, until the symbolism became complicated, and only particular

buildings would be selected for the symbolic purpose: certain forms were reasoned from the building to the world, and conversely certain thoughts of the universe were expressed in the structure thus set apart as a little world for the House of God—a Temple.[3]

Tree worship is among the earliest human traditions in all parts of the world, and is integral to the creation mythologies of many cultures. Trees are accorded special reverence because of their numerous uses, but also because of their obvious power both as living objects and potent symbols. In many cultures, trees are even symbols of humanity itself—of our aspirations to find higher meaning in the world, our need for grounding, and of our need to do the very things that trees do: provide shelter, integrate into the material world, remain consistent amid constant cyclical change, manifest stable growth, and procreate through seeds traveling far and wide across the land.

The phallic qualities of trees are obvious and legendary, and this symbolism finds its way into every culture, whether in the Maypole, the Christmas tree, or the tree in the town square in Europe. It was common in England and later its colonies to mark town squares with oak or elm trees, which also lent their name to the towns, for example Sevenoaks in Kent. I will discuss Christmas trees and their phallic symbolism vis-à-vis the Druids later in the book. In India, it is customary for serpents and snakes, especially cobras, to live among the root systems of huge trees in the middle of villages, and they are encouraged to be there, as it is thought that they help ensure the potency and generative abilities of everyone in the village, as well as the success of their crops. It might be said that "Paradise itself was a kind of sacred grove, planted by God and given to man."[4] Indeed, there are many traditions where it is believed that all trees are descended from the tree at the center of paradise.

This "tree of life" is seen as a metaphor for the entire created world. Its branches, its leaves, and its roots are deeply embedded in the earth, and its cyclical patterns of growth throughout the seasons are representative of the vicissitudes of life on this earth. The seemingly eternal tree often lives for tens or hundreds of generations, and each one starts from a tiny seed, blowing in the winds, falling where it will.

Trees are deeply significant to us, and traces of the language of the sacred trees remain embedded in our experience of the world. Alfred Kallir's wonderful 1961 book about the origin and symbolism of the alphabet, *Sign and Design: The Psychogenetic Source of the Alphabet*,[5] makes it abundantly clear that trees are a powerful force in our oral and written language. Indeed, in his vision, all languages emerged from similar ancient sources rooted in the natural world. His analysis of the letter "T" makes it abundantly clear that this letter depicts, in a

Wrapped fertility tree, Bali

simplified way, the tree. Since Kallir's viewpoint is that early humans translated the natural powers around them into symbols that found their way into the earliest languages, it is only natural that the very foundation of this logic leads us to trees. He believes that primal humanity formed associations that remain within us, embedded in our language. It is good for us to recognize the strong reactions that these connections continue to evoke. In rediscovering this inner language, we reveal a new depth to our relationship with nature.

To Kallir, the many words that either begin with the letter "T" or contain it are vestiges of early primitive thought deriving, in various ways, from tree symbolism. For example, he believes that it was lightning and thunder in the highest trees, producing flashes of light and great crashing sounds, which evoked the most extreme power of the gods. The derivation of words such as *Zeus*, the Greek *thunder* god, or the Scandinavian *Thor* with his hammer of the gods, are words related in meaning to the Sanskrit *devās*, or nature spirits, which resulted in the Latin word for god, *Deus*. In this sense, even the day of the week we call Thursday (Thor's day), is an evocation of Thunder's Day.[6]

Pointing out that our ancestors deified trees like they deified animals, Kallir notes that, in fact, trees occupied a higher position in the hierarchy of things because they were the closest living things (with the exception of eagles) to heaven, the realm of the gods and goddesses. This is also true in the sense that trees also link the gods of the sky with fertility goddesses, whose realm was the earth, and everything on it and in it. What is fascinating is that the remnants of lightning crashes—the scarring of trees, the rending of huge branches—and even the echo of the thunder sounds are encapsulated in the glyphs representing tree. Their angular contours also resemble

Joseph-Daniel Guigniaut, *The Dragon and the Hesperides*, Religions de l'antiquité, 1851

spears and other weapons that were made from trees, as though there is a natural, symbolic connection between glyph and physical object. In Kallir's mind, the symbol deputizes for the archetypal concepts, so the symbol of the weapon takes on the more powerful qualities of the thunder gods with whom the tree is compared.

Kallir notes another perspective from which trees are central in the evolution of language. When we look at a sampling of early alphabets, tree shapes and specifically the "T"-shape are among the most integral and obvious, as well as the oldest, pictograms. He identifies one of the earliest symbolic representations of the tree as being the cross, which may also be the most ancient fertility symbol in ancient Asia. This symbol exists with similar meaning both in the Hebrew letter *teth*, and in the Greek *theta* and *tau*, which is a cross inscribed within a circle. And although we do not cross the capital "T," the fact that we still cross the lowercase "t" remains.[7]

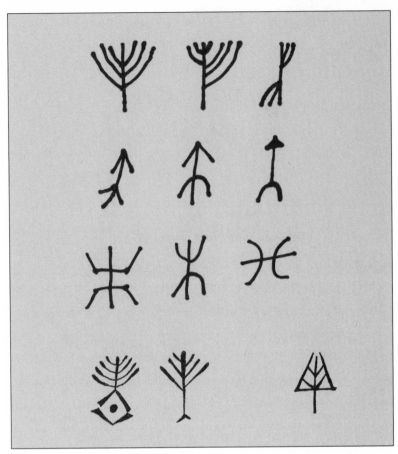

Early tree symbols and runes (after Kallir)

There is also a strong connection between these pictograms and the ancient religion of the Druids. According to an eighteenth-century source, the Druids would take the highest and most powerful tree in their area and twist its branches, rejoining them at the highest point of the tree. After this procedure, the tree took on the shape of a cross, more specifically the "tau" cross. The Druid word for *god* was *thau*, and they typically inscribed this character prominently in the bark of the tree at ground level to designate the tree as sacred. Even the derivation of the word *Druid* is connected to the tree, and may even have meant *tree*.[8] In Kallir's mind this connection to trees was central to the powerful natural magic of the northern European Druidic cults, whose mastery of arboreal environments was well-known. By ritually entwining the highest branches, they combined many magical acts—placating the tree

Joseph Martin Kronheim, *Druids of Ole England*, 1868

gods, creating and reinforcing the cross, symbolizing fertility and centeredness in the tree itself—thereby linking the tree with their belief system. This also gave the tree its rightful name, spelled in its very physical form.

The Druids exercised a kind of magic that is truly the language of sacred trees, linking the audible and symbolic meanings of the characters for "tree." The symbolic letter that signifies the tree and also the shape of that letter is echoed in the sounds of the letter as well, so we find the "T" and "TH" sounds prominent in the names of many musical instruments, through what Kallir calls humanity's "acoustic imagination." These sounds and their associated letters manifest as percussion instruments like the Indian *tabla*, the *tom-tom*, the *tamboura*, the *tympanon* (a kind of German drum), and even a part of the ear, the *tympanum*.[9] The cylindrical shapes of many instruments derive from tree roots and are also often made out of wood. Of course there are also wind instruments like the tuba, the trumpet, and others that capture and release the magical and powerful sounds of wind, thunder, and lightning in the most dramatic moments in music—from classical symphonies to rock and roll—to this day. Thus the tree is inexorably linked to the storm.

Kallir also remarks on the curious concept of the sequence of letters in European languages, which is derived from the earliest Semitic alphabets. What is especially fascinating is the hard "end" sound in the earliest Semitic alphabets is the letter "T," as the first letter of the Greek word *telos*, which for most alphabets is the letter "T," as in Greek *telos* means the end, as does *tau* in Hebrew. Although other letters were added past "T," this letter remains the strongest final sound. In a way, this shows that the significance of the trees and their unique language are either an ending or an embarkation point for something higher and more profound. The "T," of *tower* or *steer*, or the word *talisman*, signifies both "termination," but also the "initiation into a mystery." Trees and their symbols record and symbolize the upward growth that humanity can experience during times of discovery and enlightenment, as well as the tumbling down it weathers during periods of turmoil. The shape of tree symbols serve as a visual reflection of the cyclical process of civilization.

The development of sounds, symbols, and the alphabet has gone through distinct, traceable stages throughout the evolution of humanity. This process is repeated in the early development of every single human child as they learn language. It is Kallir's sense that the alphabet is a psychogenetic process. According to Kallir, language sounds reflect experiential issues and that the languages developed with such sounds as essential form factors. By postulating that the "T" sounds were at the end of the scale of alphabet values, all language skills evolve toward the horizontal stroke that crosses the letter "T," because in the early learning process children cannot easily pronounce "T." This gives rise to the later letters of the alphabet, the letters beyond "T."

In his 2004 book *The Secret Teachings of Plants: The Intelligence of the Heart in the Direct Perception of Nature*, Stephen Harrod Buhner says the following about the communication with trees and the plant world:

> Everything that you experience with the plant as you sit with it is important and bears some relation to its uses as medicine, its function in the ecosystem, its own life history and desires, and its relationship to humans and the world around it. Some of this may come powerfully in words, some only through a general sense of something that you may have more difficulty defining.[10]

A direct perception of and communication with the plant world is available to us—through our heart rather than our mind or language. Indeed, in our modern world, we are taught to think conceptually about nature, a habit that our society, especially in its modern scientific paradigm of the natural world, is inclined to accept as the only valid way to think. However, categorizing and "explaining" nature totally misses the essential point, which is that we have much to learn from nature directly. This can only happen if we are open to the languages of nature, transmitted through the natural sounds of animals and plants, and also through the substances that we ingest, smell, and use as medicines or psychotropic drugs. Yet even if we have the instinct and inclination, we don't always listen in the ways that we should, but rather tend to see nature as mute, an exhibition to be observed and studied, rather than a critical element of and participant in the very consciousness of our planet Earth.

When we look at trees and reflexively consider their material value, we may also find ourselves astonished at how many other more integral psychological and spiritual connections they present. Trees show us that if we can only learn to listen, respond to, and eventually understand their words, we will have access to a profound and essential language available to all. This book is written with reverence for all I have learned from trees: from being in them, from being around them, and from my task of sustaining the mystery and power of trees. Through this book, I hope to awaken new possibilities and ways of communicating with the spirit of our world of trees and nature.

Die and be buried who will,
I mean to live here still;
My nature grows ever more young
The primitive pines among.

—Henry David Thoreau, "Ktaddn," 1846

Trees, Ecology, and Our Fate

And so now it is the dry branches, not the green, of the universal tree around
which the heavens spin that must be grasped and painfully climbed.
—Joseph Campbell, *The Masks of God* (1968)

There is little doubt that at this point in history the relationship between humanity and our planet Earth is not only strained, but in dire need of reassessment. This process will, almost by definition, force us to change our ways or risk total destruction.

One of the many issues that we must understand is the role of trees in our natural world. Historically, trees have been essential to the development of civilization. Some of our earliest habitats were made from wood, and trees provided the most readily available fuel source for the fires that kept us warm and cooked our food. Wood was also used for utensils, vessels, and furniture, among other things. During the Iron and Bronze ages, trees provided the heat required to

Silhouetted branches

create the metals that changed the face of agriculture. Wood provided materials for the building of houses, for the making of villages, towns, and cities, and also for making the arms that fueled the continual wars that defined and changed the face of the world.

The forests were dotted with the tents that the nomadic peoples carried with them as they migrated during the Ice Ages, trying to survive highly changeable and difficult conditions, and wild swings in temperature that are actually very much like the weather we experience now.

When the Ice Ages ended, among the first habitations mankind created were villages built on wooden stilts over water. These existed in the Middle East, Mesopotamia, the Indus Valley, China, and Egypt. Indeed, the boats by which these habitations were accessed, defended, and maintained were also made of wood, initially hollowed-out trees and later more sophisticated canoes and boats.

John Vaillant, author of *The Golden Spruce*, talks about the ways in which Native Americans called the Haida used trees in a variety of different ways. They hollowed out logs to use as dugout canoes for whaling expeditions, war parties, and the shipping of goods around their areas of the Pacific Northwest. They also made giant canoes, sometimes as big as one hundred feet in length, out of cedar trees.[1] It has even been postulated that these massive canoes could have made the journey across the Pacific to Hawaii from British Columbia.[2] The Haida, like many of the Northwestern coastal Native American tribes, made almost everything they used from trees. Hats and baskets were woven from roots, clothing from red cedar bark. Medicines were derived from the bark, roots, and leaves of various trees, and carved totem poles from trunks that stretched up to the skies. They lived in wooden long houses the size of airplane hangars. Tribes in that region also approached their creative necessities as a form of art. Some of their constructions represent the epitome of craftsmanship, as shown by the 63-foot-long decorated Heiltsuk canoe that is in a permanent exhibition at the Museum of Natural History in New York. It would be fair to say that their entire culture was tied to the trees in their wonderfully fertile and wild environment. This was true in many places where indigenous peoples lived in close concord with nature and utilized natural materials for their every need. I believe that this deep and profound connection with trees remains encoded within us all, as our ancestors lived among, worked with, survived because of, and ultimately revered trees. I also believe that it is essential that we respect and express this reverence beyond passively enjoying the "look" of nature from our windows.

~~~~~

Traveling across the rivers, lakes, and seas that abound on our vibrant planet, it was essential for indigenous people to use trees to make boats. As time passed, these vessels became larger and larger, more and more capable of navigating around the entire globe. The ships of the early Chinese emperors, the Vikings, the European explorers, the Pilgrims, and even those voyagers who traversed the seas into the twentieth century were made primarily of wood. The first airplanes were wooden, and many decades after the first flight of the Wright Brothers, in 1947 the entrepreneur and visionary Howard Hughes created and built the largest wooden flying ship of all, the *Spruce Goose*. With a length of 218 feet, a wingspan of 320 feet (for comparison, the new Boeing Dreamliner has a wingspan of 182 feet) and a height of 79 feet, the *Spruce Goose* is still the largest airplane ever created. Unfortunately it had one lone flight, covering over one mile, and lasting just one minute.

Just as trees were used to create vehicles for physically conveying our ancestors around the globe, wood similarly enabled writing, in the creation of paper. A powerful medium for conveying thought, religious beliefs, and sacred works, it is paper that our literary history depends on and allows us to understand and communicate with each other on a global scale. Writing paper, paper towels, toilet paper, and the myriad other products derived from trees are necessities that continue to be required in our day-to-day life. It is impossible to underestimate the role of trees and the many products they have provided throughout the history of the civilized world.

A Disappearing Critical Resource

The Golden Spruce by John Vaillant tells a powerful story about the ravaging of the environment in an area that we don't often hear about. The Pacific Northwest is a rainforest stretching more than a thousand miles from California to Alaska. It includes a corridor of dense, high-growth forests, with some trees reaching heights of more than 300 feet. What is astonishing is that this rainforest is the largest ecosystem by weight anywhere in the world, even larger than the Amazonian Basin equatorial jungle.[3] It is virtually an alien landscape, so thick and lush with trees and other growth that it is almost impenetrable. As a result, only the edges of this immense region are inhabited.

At one time, such old-growth forests existed on all the continents, including places such as Japan, the British Isles, Iceland, Europe,

Branches of old-growth trees reaching to the sky

central Asia, and the eastern shore of the Black Sea. The only places on earth where such environments still exist, apart from the Pacific Northwest—albeit in much smaller form—are Chile, Tasmania, and the South Island of New Zealand.

These coastal rainforests are extremely fertile and the source of a great variety of life. Creatures of all sizes, especially tiny ones, live in their depths, and "It has been estimated that one square meter of temperate forest soil could contain as many as two million creatures representing a thousand species."[4] However, the tree variety most notable within this climatic paradise is the Sitka spruce, which can live up to eight hundred years, reaches heights of three hundred feet (close to that of a redwood), and can weigh three hundred tons.

Although the subject of Vaillant's book is deforestation on our continent, it is really about one particular spruce in British Columbia, a sixteen-story-tall golden spruce (*Picea sitchensis 'Aurea'*). A biologically abnormal tree in that its leaves are golden rather than green, it was gigantic in size. Because of its striking and unusual color, the local Native Americans worshipped this tree and endowed it with many myths and legends. In most of these tales, the spruce is actually a human being who had been transformed into a tree. Vaillant's book is about a crazed environmental activist desperate for a potent message to send to those who are destroying this precious resource, as well as the natural environment on a larger scale. In protest, the environmentalist cut down the massive tree. He then disappeared. Beyond the overarching narrative, the core of *The Golden Spruce* is a depiction of the way in which we in the modern world have harmed—and continue to destroy—the precious legacy of old-growth forests.

What began in early history as a need for trees to satisfy immediate necessities for food, shelter, and clothing later evolved to match humans' expanding desires. One desire that proved problematic concerned the masts of the tall ships that roamed the world in the sixteenth to the nineteenth centuries. Tall trees were needed to construct these masts. By 1605, the British, having already reduced their homeland from dense forest to meadows in just five hundred years, had begun to exploit the Northeast of the New World for the wood necessary to equip their navy. This new trove of tall pine trees was of such extreme political and military value that "a forest of straight, sturdy pine was as valuable as an oil field or uranium mine today."[5] The British Crown even designated all trees above a certain size the property of the King. The early North American logging industry was so important that when the colonies eventually began creating and circulating their own money, the designs inevitably incorporated trees such as pine, oak, and willow as symbols of the primary wealth of the land. Oaks were especially important, as they were often the sites of important agreements, contracts, and government offices. The maple leaf remains the emblem of the flag of Canada.

The first settlers in the New World were terrified by the immense forests that stretched from coast to coast and were full of wild game but also predatory animals like bears, mountain lions, and wolves. They had been used to the relative comfort of European grasslands, long denuded of large and dense forests. In the New World, seemingly endless forests surrounded the few spaces cleared by the Native Americans, creating deep fears in the settlers. It is still possible to sense this feeling of isolation today. Driving north from New York City along either side of the Hudson River Valley, one sees only the

Redwoods in California

odd village or town peeking through the dense forests that stretch as far as the eye can see. The difference is that today those endless forests are new growth, as all of the ancient trees prized by European settlers in the New World were razed long ago. We have essentially clear-cut our entire continent, with the exception of those few areas of the West Coast where redwoods and cedars still abound in their protected national parks. (Thank goodness for John Muir and Theodore Roosevelt.[6])

The history of humanity is filled with instances in which societies around the globe used trees and their valuable wood for survival. The Middle East, which we tend to think of as arid and filled with vast deserts, was once covered with trees. This was particularly true in ancient Lebanon, whose famous cedars grew dense and thick.[7] An incalculable amount of wood has been logged, sold, and used in the course of human history, which has radically transformed the face of the planet. In the mere four hundred years since North America was settled, we have transformed our once vast, tree-covered wilderness into a patchwork pattern of farmlands.

Even during the 1600s, Vaillant explains, the Europeans were logging the entire continent. By 1840 there were more than thirty thousand sawmills and other wood processing factories across the United States, using circular saws to turn the trees into rawmaterials for shipping and construction. In the decade after 1850 alone, more than 60,000 square miles of North American forests were felled and cleared.[8] Our society may decry the clear-cutting of Amazonian rainforests, yet we denuded our own continent even before the invention of paper bags or toilet paper. Thoreau talks about the many lumber mills along the Maine coast in his time. Ships had difficulties navigating because of all the scrap wood floating in the sea, having escaped the mills on land.[9]

Vaillant describes the devastation typical of commercial logging in the United States and Canada in blunt terms. While the logging companies claimed—and continue to claim—that they replant the old-growth forests they are harvesting, in reality they do not. The scene of the woods after the loggers have left is stark. Known as 'harvests' in the timber industry, they are shocking things to behold: traumatized landscapes of harrowed earth and blasted timber. The devastation is often so violent and complete that if a person didn't know loggers had been through, he might wonder what sort of terrible calamity had just transpired: an earthquake? A tornado? After a few years the stumps tend to bleach out, giving the impression of headstones in a vast, neglected graveyard. Such scenes can be found throughout the Pacific Northwest, though today many of them are artfully hidden from public view by thin screens—"beauty strips"—of spared forest.[10]

What is probably worse is that few people even know that this has happened in relatively recent history. While we have consumed, and continue to consume, the products of this atrocity, we remain ignorant of the results. The protagonist of Vaillant's book writes many extreme tracts about the wholesale destruction of the trees in the Pacific Northwest. At one point he likens the actions of the forest industry in British Columbia (primarily controlled by American companies) as an example of "economic remote controlled TERRORISM, on this planet, with professionals leading in the way in 'severe symptoms of denial, that there is any problem.'"[11]

Three Men in a Devastated Forest, logging in Cascade Mountains near Seattle, Washington, 1906

3

Symbolism of the Tree

The tree which moves some to tears of joy is in the eyes of others only a green thing which stands in the way. Some see Nature all ridicule and deformity . . . and some scarce see Nature at all. But to the eyes of the man of imagination, Nature is Imagination itself.
—William Blake, *The Letters of William Blake* (1799)

THE WORSHIP OF TREES WAS prevalent in the ancient world. Trees stood in for the divinities of the elements of nature, or as Nature herself. The first temples were sanctuaries embedded in nature, under the wide spread of prominent trees such as grand oaks or elms, which were decorated with bands of cloth, colored with dyes, and left open to the dome of the sky. Before temples became solid and immovable architecture, they were often stands or groves of trees. Worshippers gathered in clearings that were safe places amidst the primeval forests that covered much of the world.

Albrecht Dürer, *Adam and Eve*, 1504

Antonio del Pollaiolo, *Apollo and Daphne*, late 15th century

Originally, temples were dwelling places of the gods or goddesses, who were present in the temples as mystic symbols, or they would channel their messages through oracles in order to speak to their worshippers. Oracular centers like Delphi were open to the sky, and they contained symbols—in this case a cleft in the rock, a ritual cave, and a spring—that showed others that the site was inhabited by a divinity. Early humanity recognized the sacred in natural places. Initially, they looked for spiritual intervention from the sky, but in time they also found representations of the heavens, gods, and goddesses in trees, beside streams, inside caves, and eventually in tents or buildings devoted to the sacred.

Trees appear not only in ancient creation myths, but they also populate folk tales, stories, and legends from all over the world. Trees stretch up into heaven and down into the darkness of the deepest earth, making them a natural symbol for humanity's relationship to the deities, but also to the human psyche itself. This is undoubtedly why the "family tree" or the "tree of life" is such a powerful and evocative image—they are so clear and obvious, deep down, that they don't even really need to be explained. But when we explore the deeper history and mythology of trees, we see that this association is ancient, and maybe among the deepest and most powerfully evocative stories of all. Author J. R. R. Tolkien (whose stories are strongly based on earlier Scandinavian and Middle Eastern legends and creation mythologies), in his *The Lord of the Rings* series, created mythic characters like the Ents, who are wise and wandering ancient tree creatures.

A primary image at the core of many religions and belief systems is that of a paradise depicted as a grove of beautiful and strong trees growing deeply into the earth and stretching their branches and leaves

Scandinavian Yggdrasil world tree carving at Stavkirk, Norway

up into the heavens. It is one of the most natural and evocative images one can contemplate. Given that the first humans were nomadic beings who moved around incessantly in search of sustenance, it would seem that they reenvisioned the great life-sustaining trees as the trees of paradise. In Eastern religions, a natural extension of this idea is the concept that trees are a "type of universe, and represent the whole system of created things, but more frequently as a tree of life."[1]

This belief is similar to the way in which the sky was seen, because of our visual sense, quite literally as heaven, the home of the gods. The arc of the sky is a paradox; because it seems like a symmetrical dome that moves with us as we travel about the earth's surface. This gives us the sense—although it is really an illusion—that wherever we are is the center of the world. This center moves with us, and therefore we perceive that we always at the center of the world, if not of the universe—a persistent early myth in itself. Incidentally, this mythology wasn't disproved until the last few hundred years with the aid of telescopes and astronomy. The commonly accepted worldview until the time of Galileo, Copernicus, and Giordano Bruno was earth-centered, rather then heliocentric. The Catholic Church persisted in the belief that the earth was the center of creation through the Protestant Reformation and only later reluctantly admitted that this was not the reality of things.

All the stars and planets revolve around the Pole Star in the northern hemisphere, and so the Pole Star seemed to people in that part of the world to be in a fixed direction, to the north. Indeed, Ursa Major, the Great Bear, was a prominent constellation in most cultures because it pointed directly to the North Star. The earth's axis was seen as a kind of divine tent pole, and later came to be known as the Axis Mundi, or "axis of the world." It was likened to a great millstone, rotating and thus generating reality.[2] This divine axis was simultaneously where we were, and also the true center of the world. And every individual tent pole was the center of its world also.

In Scandinavian and Hindu conceptions of the creation of the world, the universe itself was seen as a great tree that grew from a mysterious and sacred seed in space. The tree therefore stands in for, and is equivalent to, the axis, pole, or reed around which the world moves. The rotational movement around a central axis does in fact create the yearly and precession cycles[3], and is also a prominent metaphor for the universal cycles of life, nature, and the world.[4] Whether the world tree is understood as emerging from a literal, physical seed or, in the case of Hindu and Christian creation narratives, emerging from the "word," the tangible world is often understood as having emerged from the intangible in the form of a tree.

In the Jewish mystical tradition of Kabbalah, the Tree of Life is represented by a diagram that shows the structure of the universe with the apex in heaven and the roots in the earth, delineated in ten stages. This is a metaphor that can also be found in Greek and Egyptian mystery traditions. Similarly, they imagined a chain of being that descended from heaven to earth, divided into various stages of development. The nineteenth-century Russian mystic and founder of the Theosophical Society, Madame Blavatsky, extended this metaphor of the world emerging from a tree structure. She asserted that the Great Pyramid was an inverted tree with the root at the apex of the pyramid and its branches at the four corners.[5]

As a child, it wasn't a great stretch for me to recognize that trees possess a connection to the divine and unknowable. It occurred to me

Alan Saret, *Because of my hair, the trees of eternity,* etching, 1984

that the trees I climbed when I was a young boy—either in the Finger Lakes of upstate New York, or in the wilds surrounding isolated freshwater lakes in Canada—were indeed centers of my world, which was itself the center of the world. It wasn't until I went out and discovered there was much more to the world beyond that initial conception that I began to question this belief. Central to Freud's psychological worldview was that, as children, our own developing conception of the world replicates the same stages of self-realization experienced by all humanity. Our childhood conceptions of being at the center of the world are similar to that of early nomadic humans, who created these ancient mythologies. The tree branches I climbed during those evenings pointed to clusters of stars, which seemed to have a kind of inherent intelligence that I needed to know about. And yet, when I attempted to communicate this fact to the people around me, no one I spoke to had a clue what I meant. My feelings about nature as embodied by trees made me feel closely connected to the natural world of life and death, more so than the omnipotent and omnipresent Christian god in heaven, who existed above and beyond the world. I found him hard to imagine, and struggled to feel a significant connection with this mysterious being.

When we grow up we begin to "understand" the world instead of feel its presence. Once our minds develop, our connection to the world and nature undergoes a shift, an abstraction of reality. We are exposed to ideas that claim to help us comprehend this reality. However, this is quite misleading, These concepts merely detach us from our own feelings and experience of reality. This disconnection is represented in ancient myths, where the gods create the human race from an ash tree with a symbolic snake surrounding its trunk, symbolizing the power of "mind." It is the serpent's temptation, symbolized by the capacity of the mind to know itself that ultimately separates us from the natural world, and on a collective level, frees humanity from the gods' power. In the Bible, this is also an expulsion from grace. In knowing our own mind, we are expelled from Eden, from intimate communion with nature. We must recapture this visceral sense of the world and regain contact with the profound magic of nature.

Dream Symbolism of the Tree

In the "Dream Symbolism of the Tree",[6] Carl Jung identifies the tree as a primary symbol of the archetypal psyche, signifying growth, depth, and enlightenment. The immense age of some trees also places them as symbols of the eternal. They are the continuity and solidity of life itself, as represented by the self.

Jung differentiated the way in which our intellect functions and another, more important, and deeper means of perception: "Beyond that there is a thinking in primordial images—in symbols that are older than historical man; which have been ingrained in him from earliest times, and eternally living, outlasting all generations, still make up the groundwork of the human psyche. It is possible to live the fullest life on when we are in harmony with these symbols; wisdom is a return to them."[7] Jung's ideas are powerful and can be challenging for us to comprehend and enact in our own psychological and spiritual development. Part of the way in which we can do this is to see the natural world as a primary source of wisdom. We can benefit from its guidance if we are able to understand its archetypal language of symbols. This isn't always easy for us to do, as it requires becoming free of our conceptual mind, and as Jung states: "Now it is the dry branches, not the free, of the universal tree around which the heavens spin that must be grasped and painfully climbed."[8]

Jung looked at old European legends and fairy tales, as well as similar lore from around the world, in addition to religious texts. He

....

"Mighty old oak; prototype of the self."

—Carl Jung

realized that there were resonances not only with the dreams of his patients, but also with the symbolism of alchemy, an ancient spiritual process by which certain individuals in many cultures attempted to achieve higher states of knowing and being. Jung considered alchemy an earlier version of modern depth psychology. The tales he studied express powerful truths that tap into our unconscious and nonrational mind, not only as individuals, but as a species. Such stories are our *collective* history, the tales that exist within us all. These narratives have accompanied us throughout the history we have shared through our common ancestors. Jung called this layer of the human psyche the "collective unconscious," and postulated that when we reach certain crossroads in life—especially when we are emotionally and spiritually stressed or actively attempting to change our ways of being—unconscious impulses push their way through to our consciousness as archetypal images and symbols in dreams and active imagination. These impulses serve as ways of guiding us through our confusion. And although these communications are often seen as fantasies, dreams, possession, delusory ideas, psychological conditions, or even childishness, Jung was responsible for reframing such states as essential to our psychological life. Beyond that, he recognized that they provide essential access to an entire vocabulary of signals and symbols that have the potential to guide our inner life.

Often these tales either start or take place in the forest, which in itself is a powerful image to the psyche, even today. Jung describes the forest as "the place of the magic happening."[9] He compares the forest—its depths and its magic—with the sea, which is also unfathomable, dark, and mysterious. Both are symbolic of the unconscious mind, which teems with life but remains unknowable, possessing a vastness that is beyond understanding. Since trees are alive and growing, Jung identifies the fact that these symbols, like the fishes of the sea, are not only contents of the unconscious, but they are *living* contents, and therefore active and changeable. The forest contains a multitude of such contents, and is a profound, living organism from which we can learn much about ourselves if we are willing to enter it. However, we must do so at our own risk.

When interpreting the significance of trees as archetypes and myths in dreams, there are valuable and important qualities of which we should be aware. Ralph Metzner explores this in *The Well of Remembrance*, in which he states that when "dealing with the image of a tree, whether it is the tree of our personal ancestry or the evolutionary tree of life, *lower* means 'earlier,' and *roots* symbolize 'origins.'"[10] Therefore, in a story or a dream, "water at the root of the tree provides knowledge of ancestral and evolutionary origins."[11] This tells us that trees are more significant to us than they appear. As a symbol they lead to our depths and our deepest unconscious impulses, pointing us to earlier states of our being, or more primal levels of existence.

A characteristic of the forest, especially in fairy tales and dreams, is that there is usually one tree larger than all the others. This gigantic tree dominates everything around it. Perhaps this is because of its immense age or its reach, or because it is at the center of the forest, where it is darkest and most mysterious. This tree is also often an oak, seen to be the greatest of all the trees in northern Europe. The oak figures from almost all mythologies in this part of the world. Jung came to realize that the dominant tree is a center of the still-living unconscious as the core of our personality—the center of the self, as it were, around which all other aspects of our being constellate. When the hero comes upon such a tree in the huge and dark forest, he is coming into contact with an aspect of himself of which he had previously been unconscious. To say that he is unconscious signifies that he is searching for himself, that he has not yet integrated his experiences of life with his essential being. "For our hero, therefore, the tree conceals a great secret."[12] Trees and forests have the potential to disclose invaluable truths about our self.

The tree penetrates deeply into the earth, breaking up the rigid nature of the mineral realm, which to Jung symbolizes the core of the self that exists in the physical body and the material world. It is difficult for us to grasp the essence of the self as he describes it, nor can we really feel like we "own" nature and its essential character. But, in trying to gain access to this deeply buried core of our being, the "tree would then be the outward and visible sign of the realization of the self."[13] He goes on to state that not only is this core of the tree equivalent to the center of the elusive true self, but it is also the tree of life at the center of the world. It is like the tree in Eden, and is also symbolic of the Christ energy in us. Some, including many medieval and Renaissance artists, also see this tree symbol as literally signifying Jesus Christ.[14]

Remarking on a peculiarity of this metaphor, in which the tree symbolizes both the hero and the self, Jung states that the natural qualities—the unrefined aspects of our being, and the naïve and primitive nature of humanity—are consigned to the roots of the tree. Therefore, these qualities are relegated to the part furthest under the ground, deepest in the darkness of the earth. According to Jung, this signifies that it is the body to which the unformed temptations and evils we carry have been banished. This brings up a powerful and important issue that is associated with Christianity in particular—that the body and its natural needs and urges, specifically sexual urges, are seen as sinful and evil. This contradicts the essence of earlier matriarchal cultures, where expressions of sexuality and engagement with the natural world are absolutely appropriate. Indeed, they keep us in touch with nature and the spirit of the earth itself. In many folk tales from these cultures, it is only under the oak, in the darkest part of the deep forest, that the hero can really look at these more potent aspects of himself, and this is certainly a valuable metaphor for us also. We must find within ourselves and our world a psychological or spiritual center where we are safe. This safety gives us an opportunity to explore our inner world more completely, in order to find the keys to our being.

Jung states that Christianity tends to suppress these darker and more primitive aspects of the self. In the Christian world, the hope is to contain them by prohibitions, to isolate them as acts of separation. Its practices have the same intent regarding expressions of sexuality and other instincts aligned with the natural world. It is my belief that this constitutes one of the most powerful examples of the deleterious effect that the patriarchal religions have had on humanity—these beliefs divorce us from intimate contact with nature. We are kept away from the secrets of the forest, and hence our own deeper nature. Today we find our culture almost completely separated from the natural world, and in denial of our negative impact upon the environment. Instead of going straight to the heart of the matter—to the roots of the trees—we have been trained to turn away from these core issues.

Jung realized that symbols such as the tree often occur in dreams as an *archetypal* quality. This signifies a quality that is not only personal, but which is omnipresent in history. Archetypes surface in very different cultures and places, and are expressed by individuals with divergent backgrounds; however, these symbolic qualities always appear with the same or very similar meanings. This goes along with the idea that such archetypes or archetypal images are *collective*, in that they belong not to any one person or group of individuals, but to humanity as a whole. In this sense, the growth patterns of the tree, upward into the sky and also downward into the earth, are *both* characteristic of human psychological and spiritual growth. Like the tree, we must grow spiritually and also ground our intent in our actions. Jung calls this inexorable growth the "process of individuation." This is the way in which we learn to express our individuality through the choices we make in life, the actions that define us, and the qualities we manifest in our lifelong process.

In his essay on the philosophical tree, Jung provides images of the many paintings and drawings done by his patients (and by Jung himself) over several decades. It is striking that the imagery is often consistent with historical representations of trees from ancient cultures and civilizations very different from his patients' Swiss or German worlds. This shows us that the tree is simultaneously a realistic object that we may see every day of our lives, as well as a symbol that we continually express and discover in a wide variety of forms. We invest both the real tree and the symbolic tree with similar meanings. Both representations of the tree connect what is above (consciousness) with what is below (the unconscious). Both have the capacity to link heaven and earth, and carry with them the idea of growth, as well as the cyclic qualities of trees that manifest their changes throughout the yearly cycle of nature. When the tree is full of brilliant green leaves, health and growth are implicit, along with the sense of coming into one's prime of life. When the tree shows its autumn coloring and its foliage might be at its most beguiling, it also reminds us that the peak of life and growth can be very beautiful while at the same time signaling an inevitable decline. So begins the wintery process of "going inside" and becoming dormant, losing leaves and vitality. This serves as a prelude to a yearly period symbolizing death and a return to the seed.

Jung found that the detail, focus, and colors in images of trees drawn or painted by his patients indicated where their "centers" lay. Some appeared to be oriented toward the conscious, upper world of the mind, while some evidenced characteristics of the unconscious, deeper

Francesco Colonna, *La Forêt Obscure*, illustration, 1467

world beneath the surface of appearances. Those individuals whose tree was balanced between upper and lower realms, or whose trees were symmetrical in appearance, were more likely to be balanced between conscious and unconscious influences. Our progression toward our center is, for Jung, the goal of our journey into the psyche.

The primary meanings of the tree symbol are: life, unfolding of form in a physical and spiritual sense, development, growth (from below upwards and from above downwards), and the maternal aspect (protection, shade, shelter, nourishing fruits). Jung discovered that there are many modes of the tree symbol. For example, examinations of consciousness may reveal alchemical trees that bear images of the sun and moon instead of fruit. One may even find Christmas trees decorated with balls depicting the seven allegorical phases of the alchemical process for discovering enlightenment. Standing under such a tree might be the figure of Christ, Hermes, or King Sol (the sun) sitting with a lion, a dragon, or a serpent. One may find the goddess Diana sitting on a whale.[15] They all symbolize the importance of finding the self through understanding the inner nature of the tree.

Some alchemical motifs suggest other uses for this universal symbol. The dead tree without leaves signifies the death of nature, the winter of the yearly cycle of growth and rebirth, and even the tree in paradise after the Fall of Adam and Eve. If the tree is shown truncated, as in Madame Blavatsky's view, it becomes a coffin or container for what is no longer alive in us. Sometimes it is what grows on the tree that determines its significance, like the golden apples of the Hesperides in Greek myth being associated with "love." The various fruits of the tree can lead the human soul out of darkness and into the light.

Taddeo Gaddi, Jesus crucified on tree of life, *Last Supper*, Basilica of Santa Croce, Florence, 1350

Where the tree grows is also an important dynamic. Sometimes the tree grows at the apex of a mountain, showing us that we must take a heavenly journey, literally or symbolically. This could be the journey of the primitive shaman to the worlds above or below. Similarly, the tree might be shown as growing in a walled-in garden, as was often the case in alchemical diagrams. This was indicative of a separate space, a protected domain in which a psychological transformation could take place. The protected place was sometimes called the "Garden of the Philosophers."[16]

Jung mentions that the tree symbol is predominantly feminine and maternal, as shown by the symbolism of the Melusina, a numinous snake or tree goddess from alchemical manuscripts dating back six hundred years.[17] She is most often shown as a crowned woman, often naked, rooted to the ground. Her hands are branches, and her fingers the leaves of the tree, ripe with fruits and glowing with her fertile energies. She can also have either a sword or branches in her

Julius Hübner, *The Fair Melusine*, 1844

outstretched hands. Jung sees associations with the Virgin Mary; with the Egyptian vegetation goddess Isis; as well as with the Buddha Sakymuni's mother Maya, who gave birth to him under a holy tree; and even with Eve. The tree (and the snake) signify wisdom, particularly the feminine wisdom named Sapientia; being under the tree can bring profound and spiritual wisdom to the one who asks for it. "For thence [from the tree] cometh wisdom," an early Latin manuscript states.[18]

Jung notes that there is a strong symbolic association between tree and serpent, which manifests in positive and beneficial ways. We see this represented very clearly in Michelangelo's Sistine Chapel painting of Eve, in which a snake's body wraps around the tree of good and evil in Eden. Church doctrine condemns Eve and the serpent; however, this is a reversal of traditional understanding, because the serpent was also an ancient symbol for feminine wisdom, the mind, intelligence, and generative power. Although disdained by the later patriarchal cultures and religions, serpent symbols remain in many forms such as the caduceus, the symbol of the medical profession.

These associations of trees are deep and profound, and lead us to understand that such overarching symbols signify the "gnosis," or wisdom component, of universal spirit. They also signify women, mankind, the realized individual (Buddha, Odin, Christ, etc.), the transformation process, the axis that connects worlds above and below, and the intersection of spirit and earth. Jung observed that when his patients reached times of change in the course of their therapy and their lives, they tended to receive symbols of the tree in various forms. Concurrently, they experienced situations that reflected their needs and aspirations and provided clues to the next stage of their development and a foretaste of their potential wisdom.

Christmas Trees Celebrate
the Winter Solstice

To the Celts, every mountain, tree, river, and spring had its own spirit. Trees in particular were revered as symbols of winter, the season of death, yet they are also representative of the subsequent rebirth of nature and the year. The modern phenomenon of Christmas trees resonates with earlier festivals of the world tree. Like those pagan festivals, Christmas takes place around the Winter Solstice, which is the darkest day of the year, as well as the anniversary of the birth of the Christ, and the turning of the year toward the light. Just as at May festivals, when virgins dance around the Maypole, elves were said to dance around the tree or Christmas pole, which was originally decked with candles or spheres of light. These are primary fertility festivals that signal seasonal shifts. Although the underlying spiritual component of the festivals have been largely forgotten, both are clearly festivals of the sacred tree.

In the ancient Middle East, the stumps of trees amidst the groves of the early Semitic goddess Asherah were used as altars. Today we see symbols of the early and original fertility worship of trees remaining in their Christianized form, together with ancient fertility symbols such as the phallus, testes, and semen. These symbols morphed into the Christmas pole or tree, the balls or decorations on the tree, and the tinsel draped over it, complete with blinking lights. As a pagan ritual, presents placed under the tree were symbolic offerings to the gods. On Christmas, Christians make their own offerings to the baby Jesus, said to have been born on that December solstice day. The Druids collected their sacred mistletoe, integral to the Winter Solstice ritual, from the great oak trees, according to the Roman writer Pliny the

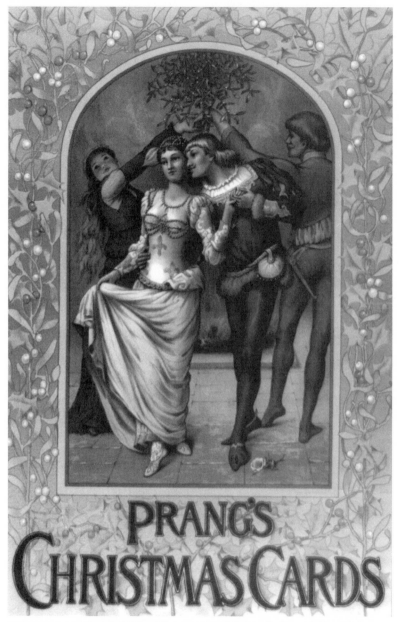

Christmas card, *Couple in Medieval Costume Under Mistletoe*, L. Prang & Co., 1886

Elder (23–79 CE). He described the ceremony thus: "They prepare a sacrifice and a holy feast under the tree … a priest dressed in white climbs the tree, cuts the mistletoe with a golden sickle, and catches it in a white cloak."[19] The symbolism is very lunar, with the dominant color white linking their actions to the moon goddess. Womb-like circular wreaths of evergreen branches characterize this ritual, as well as the sickle shape, which resonates with the moon's crescent. However, it is also a festival of Saturn, the Lord of Time, whose symbol is the holly tree. He is the old man of the North Pole. The ancient Romans always placed such "womb wreaths" of evergreens at their Saturnalias, their festivals to the god Saturn.

The eight reindeer of Santa Claus are also symbolic, as deer are sacred animals to the Druids. Deer are ruled by the moon because they reflect the light of the sun, and symbolize the eight points of the year that were celebrated as pagan festivals. The reindeer's bells resonate with the ancient tradition of ringing the bells at this time of the year. Holly trees also link modern holiday celebrations with Druidic culture, as it is their sacred tree of this season. The eight Chanukah candles also represent the festivals of the solstices and equinoxes and their intermediate points.

The god Odin is an obvious forerunner of Santa because he is a god from the Northland (Norseland). He travels on an eight-legged horse called Sleppnir, traversing the worlds of the Yggdrasil tree, of which the Christmas tree is an abstract and stylized version. The births of all the other crucified gods are celebrated at this time of the "birth of the light," at the Winter Solstice. This includes the Persian god of light, Mithras, who was born in a cave at the Winter Solstice. King Arthur was born in the great stone castle at Tintagel on this darkest of nights.

And, of course, Jesus Christ was born in the manger in Bethlehem at this time of the year. They are all "guardians of the light," who bless their trees of life at this time of the year.

In Welsh myths, oak trees are characters in themselves. They symbolize seasonal magic. Oak blossoms are used to conjure up the other magical realms, and are also connected in myth with the eagles that perch atop tall oak trees, just as the eagle sits at the apex of the sacred Yggdrasil tree in the Scandinavian cosmos.

Manley Palmer Hall mentions the old Rosicrucian doctrine that trees are not only symbolic of humanity and its wisdom, but also that they are more than abstract qualities. They designate the many highly illuminated philosophers, sages, priests, and spiritual leaders throughout history. The Druids worshipped in oak groves and were "men of the oak trees," just as Syrian wise ones were called the "cedars of Lebanon."[20] This is similar to the way in which feminine deities, wise women, or goddesses were also considered "trees" in their own right. This implies that the trees that housed the gods were literally created from, and identical to, the body of wisdom of all of the wise sages of the past.

4

HINDU SACRED TREES AND BUDDHA'S BODHI TREE

There is a fig tree
In ancient story,
The giant Ashvattha,
The everlasting,
Rooted in heaven,
Its branches earthward;
Each of its leaves
Is a song of the Vedas,
And he who knows it
Knows all the Vedas.
— BHAGAVAD GITA: *The Song of God*

IN THE CREATION MYTHS OF Hinduism, the tree was created just after the sun and moon, so it was one of the first beings to come to life after the great luminaries that signify light and darkness.[1] This

Tree goddesses, Borobudur, Java

fits with the traditional symbolism of the tree as integrating sky and earth, with its branches in the sky above and roots penetrating the soil below. One of the primary functions of the tree of the world is to sustain humanity with its fruit, very much like the trees and plants of the Garden of Eden in the Abrahamic traditions.

Sacred groves and trees were an integral part of the beliefs of people in ancient times throughout the world, and nowhere more so than in India. Stretching back to pre-agricultural times, trees have been seen as sacred entities given to humanity by the gods. There is probably no living object that is as divine as a tree to Hindus. Trees are considered to be at the highest level of the vegetable kingdom, corresponding with humanity in the realm of animals.

Apart from their intrinsic usefulness, trees of various kinds are associated with the higher powers of gods and goddesses. Some are sacred because they are used for medicinal purposes. The fact that they are by their nature phallic increases the perceived potency of trees and for this they are also worshipped.[2] Trees are similar to rice, a primary crop and integral part of the Indian diet, in that they are seen as a fertility symbol. Village trees in India are often adorned with rice offerings to designate them as fertility objects worthy of veneration.

Hindus in the rural countryside live in a world full of divine and semidivine beings: tree spirits (*yakshas* or the female *yakshinis*), ghosts, and gods (local, personal, and ancestral), all of which co-exist in a complex hierarchy. Since there is such an intimate and ancient connection between trees and the gods and goddesses, it is not surprising that there are strong associations between certain trees and specific deities, both in idea and in practice. For example, the *asvattah* or *peepul* tree (a tree of the fig family, *Ficus religiosa*), is sacred to the

Painted sacred tree, India

creator god Vishnu. In ceremonies dedicated to Vishnu, this tree's twigs are often burned as an incense, accompanied by the recitation of mantras and other prayers that are believed to direct the healing powers of the tree (and its god) by psychologically healing as well as purifying the atmosphere.

Many Indian tree varieties are used for incense, which is an important component of Hindu, Jain, and Buddhist rites and rituals, usually accompanied by voiced mantras. Five of the species of tree branches recommended for use as incense are banyan, *gel*, mango, *pakur*, and *peepul*. The mantras used in connection with these incenses help purify the immediate environment and direct the healing energies of the plants. Indeed, many such incense plants and mantras are also integral to the Hindu healing herbal technique which is a component of Ayurveda, derived from the sacred texts, the Vedas.[4]

Some of these varieties are considered "family" trees, not to confuse this term with the phrase used in genealogy. These family, or *Kula*, trees are a particular variety that is associated with a specific human family. One can see such family trees all over India in the courtyards of houses, their trunks colored with red vermillion paint, their roots or bark painted white. They may be draped with cloth, string, and various objects either enwrapped or simply hanging from the tree, as though the tree is a member in good standing of the family. And because these trees are on their property, members of this family can never destroy the trees, sometimes for generations. This is a unique Indian method of environmental conservation.[5]

....

IT IS TRUE, O BEST OF TREES, O PEEPUL TREE,
THAT YOU ENHANCE THE NOBLEST PATH
WITH YOUR HEIGHT AND THINK-LEAVED SHADE;
WHAT'S MORE, THAT YOU ARE ONE OF VISHNU'S BODIES.
—Allegorical epigram by Salikanatha Misra (ninth century CE)

Sadhu living in a tree

The cosmic world tree of Hinduism symbolizes, like other sacred trees, the power of vegetation, universal life, potency, and immortality. Trees in general are under the auspices of Brahman, and the tree of life is, to Hindus, actually a form of Brahma called the Tree of Skambha. In Hinduism, the three main gods have many different forms, often with different names. As Brahma is the creator god, the other gods (Vishnu the sustainer and Shiva the destroyer) emanate as branches from this primary great tree, whose branches stretch over the entire universe. The forest within which the tree sits, as well as the tree itself, are actually Brahman himself. In the sacred books of the Vedas, two dovelike birds, heavenly beings that symbolize day and night, visit this tree. They alternate in influence as they fly around it. The fate of the tree and its ultimate health is associated directly with the life and health of the universe itself. Since Brahma *is* the universe, and in the Hindu cosmology universes come and go—they are created, peak, and then are destroyed—the tree is a kind of cosmic indicator of the state of the universe.

Tree worship has been active on the Indian subcontinent since the fourth millennium BCE in the Himalayas and Western India. Early cultures produced pressed seals bearing a variety of inscriptions of trees: trees from which unicorn heads emerged, trees emerging from women's wombs, and women's bodies as the hanging branches of willow trees.[6] What is fascinating about these devotions is that they consider trees to be a form of beneficent *devātas*: tree spirits which are a form of *devās*, which often literally means "goddesses." However, they are usually thought of as nature spirits animating the physical world of nature and affecting fertility and growth.

> The origin of the tree of creation (Samsara-Vriksha) is rooted in Brahman, the Supreme deity, and sends its branches downward into the phenomenal world. Heat and cold, pleasure and pain, birth and death, and all the shifting conditions of the mortal realm—these are its branches; but the origin of the tree, the Brahman, is eternally pure, unchanging, free and deathless. From the highest angelic form to the minutest atom, all created things have their origin in Him. He is the foundation of the universe. There is nothing beyond Him.[7]

Many Hindu gods are believed to take form as particular types of trees. For example, Krishna was known to take the form of the peepul tree, Rudra as an Indian fig, and Brahmā as the *palasa* tree, although each god has many attributions, and these change from region to region around India. Often Hindus plant significant trees near their houses and villages as a way of bringing the presence of the gods into their lives more actively. For example, pomegranate trees are said to bring a better choice of wife and marriage, while the *mandar* tree pleases the sun and therefore imparts vitality and improves one's strength of character.

In Hindu and Buddhist literature and holy books, it is not surprising that important stories are told under trees, that strange spiritual events happen there, that great people are born under certain kinds of trees, and that men, women, and animals live together there. Trees are places of refuge, of safety, of rest, and meditation. It is from sacred trees that saints and goddesses descend to earth and also ascend to heaven.

The fertility of trees is legendary, and Hindu women flock to their village trees to worship and to ask for fertility for themselves, their crops, and their husbands. It is customary to put sacrificial objects on trees, to wrap them in cloth, to color them with paints and washes, and to

....

THIS ANCIENT ASWATTHA TREE HAS ITS ROOT
ABOVE AND BRANCHES BELOW.
THAT IS PURE, THAT IS BRAHMAN,
THAT ALONE IS CALLED THE IMMORTAL.
ALL THE WORLDS REST IN THAT.
NONE GOES BEYOND THAT. THIS VERILY
IS THAT.
—The Upanishads, 6.1

decorate them in ceremonials to encourage their support and protection. Sometimes one can barely see the tree through all the ceremonial wrappings and fertility objects hanging from every possible branch.

Fig trees are particularly important in this respect as a symbol on the Indian subcontinent and Southeast Asia as the epitomes of fertility, which probably has to do with their ability to propagate in a multitude of ways. Since fig trees grow in a mainly horizontal direction, the branches sag onto the ground many feet away from the trunk. After resting there for several years, they sprout, generating new trees on that spot. The process continues to repeat itself as the tree covers more and more area. This is perceived as a very positive sign and is encouraged. When traveling in Indonesia, the Himalayas, or India, it is customary to see such trees spreading everywhere until it is impossible to know where the primary tree begins (if it does) and the subsidiary trees end (if they do). Figs are also nourishing, shaped like the female womb, and have what many consider to be a divine taste. All of these associations give rise to a powerful mythology that is inseparable from the reality of the tree and its real and perceived uses. It is therefore not surprising that fig leaves provided Adam and Eve's first clothing.

It is sometimes the case that fig trees are hollow inside, especially when they grow to great size. In India, a stone *lingam*, an oval river stone that mimics the male generative organ, is often placed within such trunks upon a concave stone that represents the female *yoni*. We see this combination all over India, but especially near and inside hollow fig trees. In daily ceremonials, the village people come and rub herbs, creams, foodstuffs, brightly colored paint, and all manner of materials around the tops of the lingam to ensure fertility and success.

Peepul tree with altar for offerings

The Vaastu Shastra is a thorough Hindu guide that proscribes the placement and types of trees that should be planted in relation to a house, so that their influences can work most effectively. This guide describes an early kind of tree feng shui, stating that the distribution of tree varieties can activate various qualities in the house's inhabitants when certain trees are correctly placed in one of eight directions. (The exception is apparently the mango tree, which is lucky no matter where it is relative to the house itself.) These trees are in turn worshipped in specific ways, particularly during festivals in the year that correspond to their influences. The following is a mantra (prayer) repeated before cutting twigs for a celebration of the goddess Durga:

> Om, vilva tree, most prosperous, always a favorite of Śankara, I worship the Devī, having taken away your branch, O Lord! You must not mind the pain generated by the separation of your branch. I vow to the vilva tree born on the Himālaya mountain, favorite of Parvasa and embraced by Śiva. You are auspicious in action and a favorite of Bhagavatī; for the sake of Bhawani's word, give me all success.[8]

The magnificent banyan tree is also revered throughout India because it has multiple roots and branches. Also, as in the growth of the fig tree, when its branches droop near and then onto the ground, a new tree sprouts in that place, ensuring continued virility and fertility to those nearby and those who worship the tree. One often sees banyans in the center of villages, and many people, including religious men, spend time and even live under their protective spread.

THE LEGENDARY SOMA TREE

The Aryan people were the Indo-European founders of what we know as the Indian Vedic civilization. Of all of their beliefs, the magical substance *soma* is paramount, partially because it is not known today exactly from which plant soma was derived. Soma was also one of the three major gods of the Vedas, the sacred texts revealed to the Hindus by Brahma. The Vedas portray nature as alive and potent. They possess a powerful emotional connection with people, partially because of their haunting and important hymns, which was a common format for sacred books of the time.

Soma is a tree that produces a potent, invigorating—some say intoxicating, or even hallucinogenic—juice, especially when it is taken amidst intense religious rituals involving sacrifices, feasts, singing, dancing, and revelry. Soma was simultaneously a god and a plant, a dynamic that often appears in Hindu texts. He was said to have been brought to earth by an eagle. Because of the potency and importance of the herb, it was also seen as the most important plant and indeed the lord of the plants, the generating influence of the entire plant world.

Fertility tree hung with offerings, India

At the same time, the god Soma is associated with the moon, both in Vedic culture and the Hindu culture that emerged from the Vedic. His influences wax and wane just like the moon's. A mystical beverage made from soma is also connected to the moon. The drink, *amrita*, was said to confer immortality to those who drank it. It is this quality that has led many to believe that it could have been a type of psychedelic mushroom, although there are also various substances derived from sacred trees that are psychedelic when made as a tea or mixed with other substances.

The Vedic civilization utilized sacrifice as the major dynamic of its worship, and soma was integral to this worship. Trees played a large role in associated rituals, as they were the columns against which sacrifices were made. Every town would have had a tree or symbolic column near its entrance, where sacrifices took place. The critical nature of these sacrifices can be connected to trees as seen in the following anthems of the Vedic period:

May plants, the waters and the sky
Preserve us, and woods
And mountains with their trees for tresses.
— Rigveda, V,41.11

And:

Up from here have stridden three—tiger, man, wolf; since hey! Go the rivers, hey! The divine forest tree. Hey! Let the foes bow.
— Atharvaveda, IV, 3.1[12]

For both Hindu and Buddhist cultures, the ultimate symbol in art and religion was the lotus. The lotus appeared as a flower of life blossoming on earth, but also as the vehicle from which the most deeply powerful gods and goddesses arose. Even the cosmos originally emerged from a lotus flower, as "Kalpa-vrikṣa was churned as a jewel from the ocean." In imagery such as the "lineage tree" of Padmasambhava, the lotus is represented as a tree growing up out of a sacred lake.

There is a long tradition of environmentalism in India that goes beyond a simple reverence of trees for symbolic or religious reasons. Since the forests are the source of livelihood for many millions of Indians in rural areas, they have created and maintained customs that protect forested areas from destruction. There is a Rajasthani sect called the Bishnois who are "proud and aggressive environmentalists who attack those who violate their rules of ecological conservation."[13]

In India there are even trees called *Kalpa-vrikṣa* that are considered to meet all human needs, in the sense that they provide wood and shade, are symbols of fertility, often incorporate altars, provide a center for the village and a place for holy men to live, and serve many other functions as well. In Indian myths this tree is a wish-fulfilling divinity, and is said to be made of gold and precious stones. The leaves of the tree possess healing properties that are considered magical as well as

....

IT IS THE SYMBOL OF MIND, WHERE KALPA [A TYPE OF TREE]
SIGNIFIES "THOUGHT" OR IDEA. WHAT ONE WISHES UNDER THE
KALPA-VRIKṢA TREE, ONE OBTAINS.[9]

efficacious. Trees that are designated for this purpose are baobob trees, marked by smears of vermillion and myriad colored strings and scarves around their bases, as well as on those branches that arc over toward the ground. You can see these trees in the center of villages all over Southeast Asia, and every task imaginable is pursued under their shade. As the recipients of such reverence, they are participants in the sanctity of the village itself.[10]

The English fashion photographer Martin Brading has traveled to India for decades and documented sacred trees all over the country. His photographs are quite striking, showing the wildly varying places where one can find sacred trees, as well as the extent to which they are an integral part of Indian religious life. He is particularly interested in the connections between sacred trees and Shivaite cults in India. Because of sacred trees' association with snakes and serpents, which are sacred to Shiva, cobras are encouraged to live within their root system, even when they are in the center of villages with people walking by daily. Similarly the *sadhus*, holy men who are often followers of Shiva and carry the trident that is symbolic of his worship, often live around the roots or in the branches of these same sacred trees. Just as the village people make offerings to the trees, they also afford the holy men the same deference.

The serpent deities associated with trees are called the *nagas*. They are a race of serpents whose origins are described in the sacred books of the *Mahabharata* and the *Puranas*, books said to be from the dawn of time. It is common not only to see snakes living in tree roots, but also to see symbols of the Naga cults everywhere, as they overlap and interact with the Shiva cults and their *sadhus*. In some images of the Shivaite trident, you see intertwined snakes. These are similar in

Balinese tree temple

appearance to the caduceus, the later symbol for the Roman healing god Mercury, and still form the symbol of the medical profession in the west. The tridents remind us, in the same way, of the potency of such cults. Underneath their threatening outward forms, *nagas* are essentially fertility deities. Therefore, women and men from villages make devotions to the Naga trees so that the fertility of their families and fields are assured. The practice of making offerings to fertility deities is an integral part of Hindu worship and happens in a wide variety of forms all over the Indian subcontinent.

As we see in some of Brading's photos, another custom is that villagers encourage termites to create their nests—which are often as strong as concrete—around the base of trees. This is especially prevalent in village squares, probably because the nests attract snakes. These termite nests can be gigantic and look like they might threaten the health and stability of the trees. However, the trees seem to tolerate the proliferation of nests and even encourage their growth. In reality, one of the reasons behind this widespread custom is that the termite nests, anthills, and snake burrows all appear to the Hindu or Buddhist mind as entrances to the underworld. In many villages, sacred trees and

NOW COME THE DAYS OF CHANGING BEAUTY,
OF SUMMER'S PARTING AS THE MONSOON COMES,
WHEN THE EASTERN GALES COME DRIVING IN,
PERFUMED WITH BLOSSOMING ARJUNA AND SAL TREES,
TOSSING THE CLOUDS AS SMOOTH AND DARK AS SAPPHIRES;
DAYS THAT ARE SWEET WITH THE SMELL OF RAIN-SOAKED EARTH.
—Bhavabhuti, Sanskrit Poetry [16]

their termite mounds or anthills are surrounded on three sides by short walls. Alternately, villagers may thatch huts over them, or wrap fabrics around them to identify them as sacred trees. Offerings of milk or eggs are left near such shrines and they are decorated with snakestones, which are small river stones decorated with either carved or painted images of serpents or the snake virgin Nakamal. It is thought that this practice encourages fertility and success in marriage and childbearing, as well as for the village as a whole.

In Buddhism, a similar symbolism pervades the miraculous births of special beings, especially that of the great Tibetan Buddhist saint Padmasambhava, whose name means the "Lotus-Born."

THE BUDDHA'S TREES

Trees played an integral part in the life of the Buddha. It is known that the Buddha had more than one hundred and fifty incarnations before his incarnation as the Buddha Sakyamuni, and that forty-three of those times he was a deva, or female tree spirit. Trees play a powerful role in the entire life of the Buddha, from his birth to his enlightenment to his death. It is written that "The trees associated with the birth of the Buddha are Sala, Asoka, and Plaksa. Gautama got enlightenment under the friendly shade of a Pipal tree which was henceforth called the Bodhi-tree, and he died in a grove of Sala trees."[17]

....

AS THE BUDDHA LAY THERE ON HIS DEATH BED WITH
HIS HEAD FACING NORTH, PETALS FROM THE SAL TREE
BEGAN TO FALL GENTLY ONTO HIM.[11]
Christopher Titmuss, *The Awakened Life*

Balinese children with Banyan tree

At the moment of the Buddha's birth, his mother Maya held onto the supple branches of blooming *sala* trees. The moment the Buddha was born, he leapt onto the ground, and where he first touched the earth a lotus bloomed instantly.

The Buddha achieved enlightenment by sitting under the sheltering peepul tree. This tree at Bodh Gaya in India, which subsequently became known as the Bodhi tree (signifying enlightenment), has since been immortalized by Buddhists as the tree of knowledge. Myths state, among many variations, that the bark never changed color and the leaves never withered. But at every anniversary of the Nirvana day—when the Buddha achieved enlightenment—the entire tree dies instantly, simultaneously reviving as healthy as it was before.[12] The seeds from this tree were taken away, and have subsequently been planted at various sacred locations all around India.

The great Buddhist monument at Borobudur in Eastern Java is an amazing three-dimensional mandala made of stone. It is surmounted

....

THE BUDDHA IN THE MIND IS LIKE A FRAGRANCE IN A TREE.
THE BUDDHA COMES FROM A MIND FREE OF SUFFERING,
JUST AS A FRAGRANCE COMES FROM A TREE FREE OF DECAY.
THERE'S NO FRAGRANCE WITHOUT A TREE AND
NO BUDDHA WITHOUT THE MIND.
IF THERE'S A FRAGRANCE WITHOUT A TREE
IT'S A DIFFERENT FRAGRANCE.
IF THERE'S A BUDDHA WITHOUT YOUR MIND,
IT'S A DIFFERENT BUDDHA.
—The Teachings of Bodhidharma [13]

by more than five hundred life-size Buddhas, as well as more than 2,672 relief panels carved in stone, which depict the many events in the various incarnations of the Buddha. The temple represents one of the furthest movements of Buddhism to the east in the eighth century CE. It is also surrounded by four active volcanoes. Soon after construction, Borobudur was completely covered by volcanic ash from the eruption of one of the nearby volcanoes, and was not rediscovered until it was found and cleared in the early nineteenth century by Thomas Raffles, a British governor of Indonesia.

Each of Borobudur's seven levels represents levels of being in the Buddhist cosmology. The stories carved in stone show critical influences in the Buddha's former lives. The entire building is a monument to the history and culture of Buddhism. It is also a virtual library of Buddhist lore and teachings, in addition to being a magnificent work of art. On the top platform is the main stupa (shrine). It is surrounded by marble

Sacred naga tree and termite mound

statues of seventy-two Buddhas, each within their own bell-shaped stupa. It is fascinating that many of the relief panels show the Buddha symbolically linked to trees.

The Buddha predicted the birth of the Tibetan Buddhist saint Padmasambhava,

Tibetan thangka showing Padmasambhava being born from a lotus

who was born from a lotus in a lake. Tibetan Buddhist iconography and thangkas often show him at the core of a tree, which represents his spiritual lineage through subsequent history. In Buddhism, lineages describe the generations of spiritual masters who transmit a tradition over long periods of time. The lineage is both a sequence of masters,

Entwined Shiva snake motif on sacred tree

. . . .

THE FOREST IS A PECULIAR ORGANISM OF UNLIMITED KINDNESS
AND BENEVOLENCE THAT MAKES NO DEMAND FOR ITS SUSTENANCE
AND EXTENDS GENEROUSLY THE PRODUCTS OF ITS LIFE ACTIVITY; IT
AFFORDS PROTECTION TO ALL BEINGS, OFFERING SHADE EVEN TO THE
AXEMAN WHO WOULD DESTROY IT.

—The Buddha Sakyamuni

and also the generation of particular teachings. In some representations of Padmasambhava, he is seen amid a beautiful mountain lake with clear waters, surrounded by lusciously rendered nature. In the middle of the lake is a Wish-Fulfilling tree whose five branches correspond to the five directions of Tibetan Buddhism (its four cardinal points and the center). The tree is covered with different flowers, each of which produces extraordinary blessed fragrances and light. Padmasambhava, the lineage teacher, embraces his feminine *dakini* (a Tantric deity) consort. He is shown in this situation because the tree is also symbolic of the lineage of Padmasambhava, and the structure of his wisdom transmission. It is also called the "refuge tree," because those who take the vows of refuge in the Buddha, the dharma (which are the laws of nature), and the sangha (which is the spiritual community of Buddhism), have access to this entire history of Buddhism. They utilize this tree as a meditation diagram, the goal of which is to create perfect body, speech, and mind.

A primary teaching of Tibetan Buddhism is that the entire range of past and future Buddhas, wisdom teachers, demons, consorts, and the environment itself are all aspects of mind. A respectful attitude that honors the devotion of Buddhism is one that is totally in harmony with nature, as it is integral to our mind. When we visualize every sentient being becoming enlightened, we are also bringing them into our meditations.

GREEN TARA OF THE ACACIA GROVE

Compassionate One who saves us from samsara! Goddess born of the tears of the Lotus-bearer, by the power of the vow of Amitabha; most loving one who strives for the benefit of others . . . I cannot describe your infinite virtues . . .[21]

The divine bodhisattva (a being who seeks enlightenment) called Tara assimilates the various characteristics of several Himalayan goddesses. This range includes images that vary from tribal snake deities to the *shakti*, or sacred energy or force of Hinduism. The Buddha Tara is a fully enlightened female being from the time of the previous Buddha, who promised to continuously return as a female bodhisattva. As such, she is a bridge between states of being and realization. There are many emanations of Tara, but she always comes into being for the benefit of sentient beings in their struggle to overcome difficulties on the path to enlightenment.

Khadiravani Tara is the "Tara of the acacia grove (or forest)," also called the "teak forest," as teak is a wood classification as well as a specific type of tree, and acacia is a kind of teak. In Tibetan Buddhist iconography, this Tara is accompanied by her attendant bodhisattvas Marici and Ekajata. Marici (meaning "goddess of light rays") is a solar goddess, and Ekajata holds a skull-cup in her left hand. The Tara is seated beneath an Ashoka tree on a lotus throne, and holding a lunar disc, symbolizing the moon. She sits in a landscape of rocks, clouds, lakes, and flowers, which identifies her as an embodiment of the feminine goddess principle. She is one of the many forms of the Green Tara, as she sits with her right leg outstretched and her left drawn in, which indicates the principle that she abhors evil defects, strives to develop positive qualities, and has abandoned the extremes of *samsara* (illusion) and *nirvana* (enlightenment). She is green, symbolizing the element of air, which stands for perfection in all ways. It is interesting to note that in Tibetan culture, the color green is considered to contain all the other colors. In fact, recent research shows that yellowish green is the part of the color spectrum to which

Sacred tree at Borobudur, Java

human visual perception is most sensitive because it is in the very middle of the visual spectrum of colors. Apparently humans are the only beings to see the color green.

The Green Tara extends her right hand in the gesture of generosity as she bestows liberation on behalf of all living beings, which is the function of the taras, and why they are so loved. Her left hand is at her heart in a protective gesture because she protects humankind from the "eight great fears." Her hands hold lotus flowers that blossom by her shoulders, symbolizing her compassionate wisdom. She appears very young and beautiful, endowed with the forty marks of an enlightened being, and wears heavenly silks, golden ornaments, and jewels.[14]

She appears in the forest as a beautiful Emerald Lady, pure and youthful, with exquisite blue-black hair and adorned with

Sacred Bodhi tree at Borobudur, Java

colored jewels. After Nagarjuna, the great Indian monk and master scholar, discovered her in the forest, he composed a prayer and dedicated it to her in his devotion. Her beauty is so profound that she tamed the fierce animals of the forest, and she is therefore seen as a source of life, solidity, permanence, and firm-rootedness. She is also known for being "rooted to the spot," and because she is a source of life, by definition, she also signifies infirmity, old age, death, and rebirth."[15]

CHALDEAN, BABYLONIAN, AND ASSYRIAN TREE MYTHS

That tree, O king, is you.
—DANIEL 4:10–22

TREE GODDESSES PROLIFERATED IN THE Middle East from late prehistory up until the first millennium BCE and beyond. They were common to almost all cultures in the region: Sumerian, Uruk/Ur, Akkadian, Babylonian and Chaldean, Assyrian, Egyptian, Canaanite, and many others. In such early times—before there were palaces, temples, mosques, or churches—sacred places were groves of trees where the people worshipped the goddesses. Worshippers conducted ceremonies that were meant to increase fertility and the growth of crops. As most of these early cultures were initially tribal and nomadic, their cult places moved around from grove to grove,

Sargon and the Sumerian tree of life

creating numerous "sacred" sites. In all the Sumerian cultures, the tree of life was a direct symbol and representation of a predominant tree goddess in that area. A bas-relief from 2500 BCE shows the tree of life goddess with two intertwined serpents next to her. For thousands of years, it was common for the snake and goddess to be depicted together, often intertwined, in this way. The connection between goddesses and snakes is ancient and profound, as both symbolize the generative principle, as well as the darkness of the underworld. Snakes nest in the darkness beneath the earth, and the goddess generates life from her womb, but both are also associated with death and wisdom. The two archetypes are interconnected in almost all early cultures throughout the world.

The Mesopotamians worshipped certain trees that were sacred to them. Their convention was to add the symbolic horns of other deities to trees. This imagery shows a plant venerated as a vegetable symbol of a divine power, like the Asherah mentioned in the Bible, or a mythical plant like the winged oak, on which a supreme God had woven the earth, the starry firmament, and the ocean. The Mesopotamian epic of Gilgamesh contains the influence of the tree goddess Ishtar. Gilgamesh and his companion Enkidu cut down a sacred cedar forest and take the tallest trees for the gateway of their capital city, Uruk. Ishtar offers to be Gilgamesh's companion and he refuses, at which she summons the gods to punish him. This epic story echoes the shift from matriarchal tree goddesses to the patriarchy, as evidenced by Gilgamesh's rejection of Ishtar and the symbolic cutting of the cedar trees.

The cults of Ishtar or Inanna in Babylonia, Isis in Egypt, and Ba'al in Canaan were tree cults in which the tree and the goddess were worshipped as one. In one of the Babylonian Epics, a tree of life is said

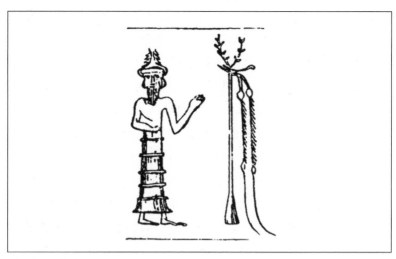

Chaldean cylinder tree goddess

to "reach by its roots the bottom of the underworld and by its top the heaven of Anu," thus identifying it as the cosmic tree.

One of the places in which the symbol of the sacred tree and specifically the tree of life was first found was in ancient Chaldea, in the fertile crescent of land between the Tigris and Euphrates rivers that is now part of Iraq. Images from this era, preserved in artifacts exhibited at museums throughout the world, frequently show a stylized tree. It is well known that there weren't many trees in that part of the world at the time, because it was only the crops irrigated by the rivers that were fertile. Those trees that endured the hot, dry, and desolate climate were most likely evergreens. These resilient trees appeared to go through the yearly cycle unchanged, as though they were eternal, which is almost certainly why they were revered.

The Chaldeans worshipped a pine tree from the forest of Eridhu, which was situated at the mouth of the Euphrates, as their tree of life; its cones were seen as being particularly significant. These pinecones were the seeds of future trees and were therefore a symbol of fertility and of the enduring power of the Chaldean kings. In cultures where the earth was revered, the powers of nature—both animal and vegetable—were thought to be from the same source. This source also endowed these powers on kings who were often worshipped as divinities. It is as though the kings claimed to inherit, take on, and maintain this power, which had been handed down through the generations in matriarchal and natural Earth mother cults. Their kingly symbols bear visual evidence of lineage, in which a current king exhibited his power by demonstrating that he had taken ownership of his predecessors' most important symbols.

Many of the representations of sacred trees from this time look more like columns with geometric patterns of branches and leaves than realistic images of a tree. This is an interesting convention, because in the Middle East to this day, many carpet patterns depict the symbolic tree of life in their geometric designs. For many of the nomadic cultures of the area, the iconography of these carpets was a primary method of delivery through which the tribe was able to preserve and communicate legends, religious beliefs, customs, and histories through generations. Therefore the tree was not only an important image, but also symbolized deeper cultural patterns.

In early clay tablets and scrolls from Assyria, we can see the tree of life represented with the early and powerful King Ashurnasirpal II (ruling from around 884–859 BCE), which marked the flourishing of neo-Assyrian figurative art. The tree appears under the winged solar disk of Ashur, the supreme god of the Assyrian empire. It was expounded particularly in the decoration of the monumental Royal Palace that the sovereign erected at the northwestern extremity of

Assyrian King Ashur anointing the tree of life

the Acropolis of Nimrod, which contained more than four hundred representations of the sacred tree. Some reliefs show the mythic symbol of the regal sacred tree. Sumerian and Babylonian creation myths show a stylized palm tree, planted by the goddess Innana, or Ishtar, upon the top of a mountain. The symbol of the regal sacred tree stretched across all of these cultures.

The Zoroastrians were an early Persian culture that had a complex cosmology based on the concept of a cyclical world, and of recurrent world ages. Their structured world time periods were very much like the Hindu *yugas*, with series of world ages associated with various precious metals. They structured their temporal universe around the image of a cosmic tree with seven branches (gold, silver, bronze, copper, tin, steel, and an iron mixture). This image is associated with

Nimrud and the Assyrian tree of life

still-earlier Chaldean ideas. These concepts were themselves influenced by Chaldean astrology, which incorporated seven known planets, including the sun and the moon. The Chaldeans' world was governed by alternating influences of a positive creator god Ohrmazd, and his destructive polar opposite Ahriman. These two gods warred constantly, generating the changes of the ages.[1]

Many of the main patriarchal religions originated in the Middle East. Early creation, fertility, and tree goddesses birthed male gods, who gradually gained ascension over them by suppression. Later, the patriarchal monotheistic religions gradually took control and their followers systematically rewrote the mythic records to eliminate any traces of these originating goddesses. It is not accidental that the feminine was subsequently associated with temptation, evil, and sexual corruption and considered a major threat to the established order, which continues to this day.

The tree goddess Asherah was the wife of El in Ugaritic (Canaanite or early Semitic cultural) mythology, and is called: "She Who Walks on (or in) the Sea." She is very similar in appearance and significance to the Arabian goddess called Al-Lat. The prefix "El" means "God," indicating that she has a godlike lineage. She was the chief goddess of Tyre in the fifteenth century BCE, and was also the wife of the god Ba'al (the son of El). Ba'al had three wives who were also his sisters: Astarte (goddess of the evening star and a mother goddess), Asherah (goddess of the sea and consort to Ba'al), and Baaltis. This was common, as in Egyptian mythology where Isis was both sister and wife of Osiris. Al-Lat was also similar to the

The Goddess Asherah

Egyptian goddess Hathoor in appearance and attributes, and both were known as the Turquoise Lady.

Asherah was a goddess of acacia trees, but she was also associated with sacred poles that were most likely representative of trees. Eventually she became the wife of Yahweh, who was a later manifestation of the lineage of El and Ba'al. Al-Lat and Yahweh were considered equal in importance. This earlier Yahweh later became the Hebrew Yahweh.

These tree cult sites were where later cultures situated their early temples and formal sacred places. The early Jewish fathers in particular were known to have erected temples near sacred groves, and churchyards throughout Europe are always adjacent to sacred groves of hemlock and oak trees.

EGYPTIAN SACRED TREES

The Ancient Egyptians revered a sacred hill. Upon its apex was a "heaven" tree, on which a sacred bird perched. The celestial waters of life came from the roots of this tree. This Egyptian "tree of life" was often represented as a date palm tree, as shown in many of the engravings and iconography in Egyptian art, as well as in their tomb paintings. Trees are important in Egyptian religion and are associated with many of the major gods and goddesses, as well as pharaohs. The god of writing, Thoth, was thought to have caused the growth of trees. In an ancient text, Thoth records the name of a pharaoh on a sacred sycamore tree.[2] Both the gods Ra and Osiris are associated with sycamore trees, as was the goddess Hathoor, who was called "the

....

IN THE TREE OF LIFE OF THE EGYPTIANS, WE HAVE PERHAPS
THE EARLIEST, CERTAINLY THE MOST COMPLETE AND CONSISTENT
REPRESENTATION OF THIS MOST ANCIENT AND SEEMINGLY UNIVERSAL
SYMBOL, OF THE TREE OF LIFE, IN THE MIDST OF PARADISE,
FURNISHING THE DIVINE SUPPORT OF IMMORTALITY.[2]

—Sinha

goddess of the sycamore." Because of this association, sycamores were often planted near necropolises, where the dead were entombed.

Sacred trees play a central role in the Egyptian mysteries of Osiris and Isis. The myth of Isis and Osiris is the central mystery in Egyptian religion, and it is suffused with tree mythology.[3] Osiris was a quasi-human god who became ruler of Egypt after the ascent of Ra, and was responsible for creating Egyptian civilization. Isis was the consort and also sister of Osiris, and was the domesticator of wheat and barley, and therefore a natural vegetation goddess in Egyptian lore. Osiris taught humanity about tending vines, making wine, and also about the domestication of the animals and plants that were so essential to the primarily agricultural Egyptian civilization along the banks of the Nile. This made his brother Typhon (or Set, the god of time, who is equivalent to Saturn) jealous, and so Set created a beautifully ornamented burial chest. It was so attractive that Osiris wanted it at all costs. Osiris climbed inside to try it out, finding that, as he had suspected, it was sized perfectly for his body. However, as Osiris was admiring the chest, Set slammed the lid shut, trapping Osiris inside. He then had his associate throw it into the river, and the chest was swept down to the sea. The chest washed up onto the shore at Tanis, and upon that spot a gigantic tamarisk (some say acacia or willow) tree grew to enclose the coffin, and entirely concealed it within its trunk.

The local king liked the tree so much that he had it cut down and it became a column of his palace. In due course, Osiris's sister Isis came looking for him. Isis found the pillar and freed Osiris, only for him to be immediately discovered by Set. Set cut Osiris into fourteen pieces, which he then hid around Egypt. Isis found each part in a different city,

Erik Ansvang, *Pharaoh Ramses and Egyptian tree of life at the Temple of Karnak*, Luxor, Egypt

and magically put Osiris back together so that they could create a child together, the sun god Horus. Each city then revered its respective body part and erected temples in honor of Osiris, who became the supreme god of the dead. Osiris' son Horus eventually captured Typhon, and the two lands of Egypt were reunited as one.

Osiris became the judge of the dead as described in the Egyptian rites written in The Egyptian Book of the Dead. He is identified with tree spirits, such as a sycamore that guards the entrance to the western Kingdom of the Dead.[4] Once a departed soul of the dead traverses many terrifying regions, it comes to this tree, out of which a tree goddess emerges to provide magic food and water for the soul's continued journey toward rebirth. In some Egyptian iconography, one can see the tree goddess portrayed as emerging from the trunk of a tree.

Egyptologist R. A. Schwaller de Lubicz, who spent years studying the Temple of Luxor, provides us with an interpretation of this myth in

The Temple of Man (1949). In his estimation, it is astronomical as well as vegetative. The myth depicts the symbolic integration of upper and lower Egypt, but it also functions as an astronomical myth, showing the relationship of the pharaoh to the universe and the Milky Way galaxy. The death and resurrection of Osiris is a metaphor for the division of the solar year (associated with his son Horus) into twelve months, which resulted in the creation of the early Egyptian calendar. However, it is also a vegetation myth in the sense that knowledge of the calendar was essential for the growth of the crops that sustained the country.

In some versions of the myth, a sacred tree of life surmounts Osiris's tomb, forming a sacred mound or hillock. This again demonstrates the primacy of tree worship in ancient Egyptian mythology. The trunk of the tree in which Osiris was first buried is an *axis mundi* (world axis), around which the starry sky revolves. The wrappings of a pharaoh's mummy, which is always symbolically Osiris, are representative of the tamarisk or acacia tree that enwrapped his body in the casket. Archaic tree and well rites were venerated at Heliopolis at the headwaters of the Nile, and trees were seen as sources of nutrition for the departed souls on their journey to everlasting life. It is also interesting and virtually an architectural paradigm that later temples used columns with floral or tree-like decoration to show this earliest root of their worship.[5]

The *uas* symbol, which is like a crooked branching symbol, was used in Pharaonic burials to signify that the pharaoh possessed the "key of the Nile." In Tutankhamun's tomb is a *uas* that shows its divine origin as a tree branch, cut along with a piece of the trunk of the tree, and entirely covered with gold. The *uas*, a living branch that is a vehicle for the ascending sap, is the lifeblood of the tree. As Lubicz explained, it "pertains to an activity, the creative function, which is not yet the created."[6]

Osiris Raising the Djed Pillar, from the Hall of Osiris in Abydos, Egypt

The early Phoenician tree goddess Astarte appears in Egypt as Qadashu, with curly hair, astride a lion, and holding lilies and serpents in her hands. She is often seen nude, wearing a hairstyle just like the goddess Hathor, who is also customarily shown carrying a lotus or a lily. She had her own oracular priests and was almost certainly worshipped in orgiastic rites. An Egyptian prayer to her in a Levantine burial ritual says:

> *Praise Qadashu, Lady of the Stars of Heaven,*
> *Mistress of All the Gods,*
> *May She grant life, welfare, prosperity, and health.*
> *Mayest thou grant that I behold thy beauty daily.*

HEBREW TREE SYMBOLISM

"But ye shall destroy their altars, break their images and cut down
their groves, for thou shalt worship no other god, for the Lord
whose name is jealous is a jealous God.
(EXODUS 34:11-16.)

TREES ARE CENTRAL ELEMENTS IN the foundation of many of the world's earliest Middle Eastern religions to the extent that *tree* is also a metaphor for *foundation*. This connection, combined with the rarity of trees in most of the arid region, contributes to their known attributes of strength and longevity, as well as their frequent usages as symbols of the sacred.

Before the Biblical exile, around the sixth century BCE, the Hebrew people worshipped Sumerian and later Canaanite goddesses such as Astarte and Asherah. They saw these idols as fertility goddesses, whose primary symbol was a sacred pole created from a stripped tree. The

Stained glass window depicting a menorah

tree was not only the goddesses' symbol, but it was synonymous with the goddesses themselves—in the case of Asherah, both the tree and goddess shared the same name. In Judges 6:25, the patriarch Gideon tells a story about the images of Ba'al and the pole of Asherah—erected in his yard, at a time when this patriarch felt challenged by the revival of such earlier cult worship:

Then Gideon cut down all of the poles (trees) from the hills around Jerusalem where the women had worshipped Asherah; in effect, the equivalent of female castration.

Six hundred years later, as told in 2 Kings 23:14, King Josiah of Judah again cut down the sacred poles, which were reminders of the sacred groves where the women held their fertility ceremonies. This action was a way of discouraging worship of the tree goddesses, who threatened the accepted primacy of the male, monotheistic Jehovah. The Old Testament prophets were diligent in their efforts to prevent the constant attempts at reversion to goddess worship. To the prophets, it seemed that when times of trial and chaos threatened, the populace

Menorah on the Arch of Titus, Rome, 82 CE.

tended to go back to their previous ways of worship, abandoning the "true" monotheistic faith. Even as late as the fifth century BCE, Yahweh and Asherah were often worshipped as a sacred couple. It is even tempting, as blasphemous as it might seem to us today, to consider her "Mrs. God."

According to the psychologist and philosopher Theodor Reik, the deep psychic need for the mother goddess among the Jewish people resulted in the Torah, which is the ultimate patriarchal device, but also happens to be a primary symbol of the maternal body.[1] In Jewish legends cited by Reik, the Torah is associated with the Tree of Life and, in a supreme irony, the two wooden spines of the Torah are typically made of *shittim* wood, known to be the tamarisk or acacia tree, the very tree sacred to the earlier goddess. Although it cannot be known for sure, it is possible that the original Tabernacle was made of acacia wood, due to its many mentions in the Bible. If this were true, it would represent another relevant use of acacia or *shittim* wood in Judaic holy objects.

In *The Symbolism of the Dream*, Freud showed that wood and other primal materials are archetypal feminine symbols; therefore, whenever the rabbis raise the scrolls of the Torah, they rejoice in a connection with the earliest origins of the word of God with Asherah as the sacred pole. Ironically, this is particularly apt as the root word *religio* means "to link back." This act of linking back is a symbolic reiteration of the cult of the primal Mother Goddess, under the auspices of the scrolls of the Law, delivered by Yahweh to Moses on the sacred Mount Sinai, in the name of the congregation of the brotherhood.

The sacred Ark of the Covenant shares a feminine and goddess-oriented origin and its symbolism is even more complex and contradictory. The Israelites carved the ark out of acacia *shittim* wood and

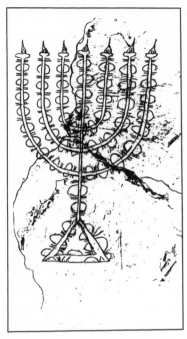

The Jerusalem menorah with a triangular base. (After sketch by Mary Rowinski.)

covered it with beaten gold. This again shows the internalization of powerful tree goddess feminine symbolism in this most sacred object, which held the Tables of the Law, and which contained an immense, almost nuclear, power.

What is also of interest is that in the traditional imagery of the ark, the two cherubim (angels) with folded wings facing each other from each end of the ark are almost certainly feminine and clearly derive from Egyptian imagery. Yet Judaism condemns any such imagery or idolatry. This is the only example of ancient Judaic tradition known to violate this cardinal law.

The process of integrating early matriarchal tree symbols into central objects of worship and veneration occurred in a pronounced way in all of the Abrahamic religions. The virulent reactions to Dan Brown's novel *The Da Vinci Code*, which postulated that Mary Magdalene was the wife of Jesus Christ and bore him a child, shows us that this issue is far from dead and buried. Not only is the suppression of the feminine a historical reality, but the symbols originally tied to the early Middle Eastern mother goddesses remain prominent within Abrahamic religions to this day, available but hidden even to the most knowledgeable scholars, rabbis, imams, and priests. By some incredible historic amnesia, many people revere these tree symbols of the feminine in their daily worship, but have no comprehension of their origins.

Contrary to the inherent patriarchal superiority of Judaism, the symbolic shape of the seven-branched menorah is a tree, although this mythic origin is rarely known or discussed in contemporary Judaism. In early representations, the menorah had a triangular base, symbolizing the feminine and the goddess. However, this has gradually disappeared over time, becoming a square platform, although it does still represent seven as a feminine number.

Tree symbolism has survived within ancient religious cultures throughout generations. For example, in the later Hebrew mystical cults, the Tree of Life has morphed from the trees of the Garden of Eden into a geometric scaffold that symbolizes the nature of the entire universe of forms. We can see an earlier manifestation of the Tree of Life in the Assyrian version of the imagery, which is surmounted by winged figures. It bears a great similarity to the Hebraic tree imagery.

THE TREE OF LIFE

The Hebrew Tree of Life is central to esoteric or mystical Judaism. It is symbolic of the path to god that echoes the earliest creation myths of Genesis, and it is therefore part of the mystical cosmology of the Kabbalah. The tree has ten *sephira*, or divine emanations of god through which he manifests creation, that symbolize the numbers one through ten. These *sephira* also represent steps from primordial unity in the symbol of *Keter*, the Crown at the top, through to manifestation on Earth with *Malkhuth*, the Bride at the bottom. While these complex, tree-inspired symbols are beautiful in structure, it is fascinating

A.T. Mann, *Hebrew Cabbalistic Tree of Life*, 1975.

that many recognize in them echoes of theories of creation studied in modern physics. You can see from the image of the Tree of Life that it embodies profound geometric beauty and magical symbolism, which is why it is revered not only by rabbis, but also within mystical Christianity, Renaissance Hermeticism, and Sufism.

Joseph Campbell, in his book *The Masks of God*, discusses how the origin of the idea of a symbolic tree of life must lie far back in history. The first great civilizations—Sumerian, Egyptian, Vedic, Buddhist, Greek, Roman, Aztec, and Chinese—created symbols of potency by orienting their capitals and temple cities toward the Pole Star, and thereby were able to orient buildings to the four cardinal directions. These civilizations and their corresponding symbols all began to gradually

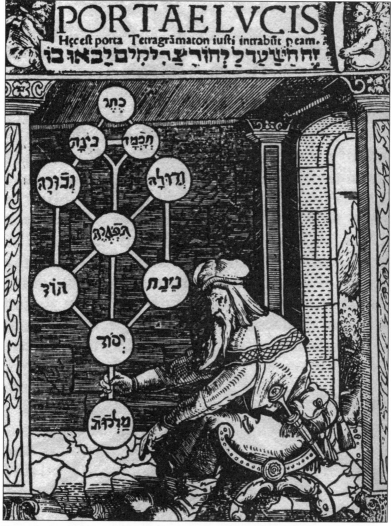

From a Latin translation of Joseph Gikatilla's influential kabbalistic work, *Portae Lucis*, 1516

merge over thousands of years, showing that cultural symbolism is often all interrelated in subtle ways. Campbell wrote, "It can be said without exaggeration that all the high civilizations of the world are to be thought of as the limbs of one great tree, whose root is in heaven."[2] He goes on to tie in the human need for celestial cosmologies, such as astrology, with buildings that reflect the connection to heaven and the gods and goddesses. These spiritual and structural configurations utilize the tree as the premier symbol of a "universal order," which is how these paths to integration came about and how the paths link together in our modern worldview.

There is also in the metaphor of the Tree of Life a cosmology and mythology that has rippled down through history since the Sumerians. In their book *Hamlet's Mill*, history professors Giorgio de Santillana and Hertha von Dechand provide a virtual litany of cultures that used the tree image to describe not only their creation mythologies, but also the key of their cosmologies. These mythical trees are something more than a "world tree," because they are all also "cosmic trees" that point the way to important ideas about the relationship of humanity to the cosmos. This book lists cultures and related images such as the tree of the cross and Christians; the Yggdrasil tree and Scandinavians; the oak and Zeus—part of which was built into the legendary ship Argo; the laurel tree at the site at the Greek Delphic oracle; Uller's yew, part of the Hamlet legend; the dark tree of Eridu in Sumerian myth; the tamarisk in Genesis; the chest of acacia or tamarisk that entombed Osiris; and the mesu tree of the Gilgamesh epic.[3] Santillana and von Dechand describe these legends and myths, which are symbolic of celestial phenomena linking heaven and earth. These trees and their correlating religious beliefs are indicative of a culture's recognition of the "underworld," because of the belief that as tree branches reach up into heaven, their roots penetrate down into the "underworld," later identified as the "unconscious" by psychologists such as Jung.

Indeed, in the Gilgamesh epic, the mes-tree of Marduk (the god equivalent to Mars) "had its roots in the wide sea, in the depths of Arallu, and its top attained High Heaven," and then "where is this mes-tree, flesh of the gods, adornment of kings?"[4] The tree seems to really be a true "tree of life" in more ways than one.

A similar tree goddess called Al-Uzza existed in pre-Islamic Arabia, where a sacred acacia was worshipped at an annual festival hung with fine clothes and ornaments.[5]

7

GREEK TREE MYTHS

*When you enter a grove peopled with ancient trees, higher than
the ordinary, and shutting out the sky with their thickly intertwined
branches, do not the stately shadows of the wood, the stillness of
the place, and the awful gloom of this doomed cavern then strike
you with the presence of a deity?*
—SENECA, ROMAN PHILOSOPHER AND DRAMATIST (4 BCE–65 CE)

MANY OF THE GREEK GODS and goddesses from Olympus were originally vegetation deities. For example, Dionysus, Demeter, Adonis, and Attis were all associated with plants in their earliest conceptions.

The god Dionysus is a goat god with cloven hooves, and is related to the god Pan, who was also shown with the small horns, furry legs, and facial features of a goat, like the satyrs with whom he reveled. Dionysus was a woodland deity, and was often called the "Lord of the

Ancient olive tree in Pelion, Greece

Wood," because he also spent time with various tree nymphs, as well as the *sileni*, wood spirits whose name is from the same root as Silvanus, a Roman deity whose name means "of the woods" in Latin. In spite of his animal attributes, though, Dionysus is primarily a tree god.

The goddess Aphrodite was born of seafoam created when Cronus severed Uranus's genitals and threw them into the ocean. She married Hephaestus, god of smiths; legend has it that she was born in a flowering orange grove amidst the Garden of the Hesperides, located either in the Libyan desert or on one of the Cape Verde islands in the Atlantic. The myth represents no less than the entrance of pure beauty into the world. It, like many myths, is connected with legends of the ancient kingdom of Atlantis.

There are also other interpretations of the apple trees of the Hesperides in Greek mythology. Sir James Frazer, the famous Scottish anthropologist, mentions a mythic ceremony that took place during ancient times in early spring, in April. A straw man representing a tree spirit is placed on the oldest apple tree in a village. Only when the first apple blossoms arrive a month later is he freed by being taken down and cast into the water. Frazer mentioned that rural and pagan people believed that vegetation deities inhabited both the fruit and the tree. They believed that the yearly return of the blossoms was intimately connected to the resurrection of nature itself, since most of the gods and goddesses themselves embodied aspects of nature. We see that the cycles of the natural world intersected so-called pagan life in every possible way, and were the true foundation of the great mysteries of classical civilization—nothing less than a celebration of and reverence for the mysteries of death and mystical rebirth applied to the year. When the adherents of the Greek mystery religions

Engraving of an early Greek cameo showing Poseidon and Athena planting the first olive tree in Athens

participated in the mythic transformations of nature embodied by the movements of the natural world, it ensured that their souls would also be reborn.

As Riane Eisler remarks in *The Chalice and the Blade*, the change of the old order of the matriarchy was signaled in many cultures by the ritual or mythic slaying of snakes by the anointed hero, as snakes symbolized feminine wisdom, healing power, and sexuality. Zeus was the slayer of the serpent Typhon. Apollo killed Python, the serpent dragon who guarded the oracle, and took over ruling

Dante wears a laurel crown in this etching by Gustav Dore from 1860

the oracle at Delphi, but retained the Pythonesses as prophetesses. Hercules killed the serpent dragon Ladon, guardian of the goddess Hera's sacred fruit tree, which was a special gift from Gaia at the time of Hera's marriage to Zeus.[1] The Middle Eastern patriarchal god Ba'al killed the sea serpent Lotan, and Jehovah killed the sea monster Leviathan, while the hero Perseus slew the sea serpent Cetus to save the enchained goddess Andromeda.

In *The Sirius Mystery*, Robert Temple talks about the Mediterranean and Asian prophetic and oracular centers, noting that the major oracle centers had a "tree-code" with which they were associated. The code was determined by the trees that were sacred to the various cult centers. He mentions that the cult center at Dodona was associated with the oak; that Delphi was associated with laurel trees; and that the palm tree was at the center of Apollo on the sacred Greek island of Delos. All of the oracular centers in Lebanon were associated with the area's famous cedars. The willow tree was connected with the cemetery at Chochus and the Circean island of Aeaea; the Omphalos (navel of the world) with the willow tree near Knossos and the island of Crete; and the cypress with the south coast of Cyprus and Akrotiri in Greece. Finally, the oracle center at Hebron was associated with the wild acacia or sant tree, which Temple equates to the "burning bush" that signified the appearance of Jehovah to Moses in the Bible.[2] Temple also mentions the interesting fact that before Apollo was the deity worshipped at Delphi, the site and cave was sacred to the Great Goddess Gaia. The eventual usurpation by Apollo was viewed as a hostile takeover by the worshippers and the inhabiting priestesses of the earlier cult center.[3]

Homer mentioned that prophetic activity at the famous shrine at Dodona in northern Greece took place under an oak tree, as the celebrants and prophets were required to sleep under the trees with unwashed feet. This fascinating, if slightly bizarre, practice is echoed in *The Ringing Cedars* series of books by Russian entrepreneur Vladimir Megre. In these books, first published in 1996, the author communicates the philosophies of a woman named Anastasia, who speaks to him as an advocate of nature. Anastasia recommends enabling a closer connection to nature through unusual methods of growing one's crops. Among other things, she recommends that we walk near plants or trees without washing our feet to communicate our healing needs to and from the natural world.[4]

Temple goes into great depth about the powerful correlation between oak trees and oracular centers. The Greek Omphalos (the symbolic center of the world to Greeks) was a short column with a rounded top. Emblazoned with strange symbols, it mimicked the spiraling path of the planets in its diagonal patterning, which reflected the ecliptic path of the planets in relation to the horizon. It was thought to be the "navel of the world," very much like the world tree as a symbol. Although the most famous Omphalos was at Delphi, there were others at Dodona, Knossos, Behdet in

The omphalos stone at the oracle in Delphi, Greece

pre-dynastic Egypt, Delos, and at the Greek island of Kythera, where an unusual calculating device—some say the first computer—was recently found. All these "navels" were also oracular centers, each with their own cults, priestesses, and rituals. Early nineteenth-century British historian Godfrey Higgins explored the deeper symbolism of such oracular cults. He discovered that the verb root of the words for "to say" and "to speak or pronounce" is the word for *oak*. The "Om" sound, which means "the speaking of Om," is part of the name "Dodona," and, literally derived, means "oracle." Temple mentions that it was common in those times to give an acorn as an offering to the Mother Earth goddess Gaia.[5]

The closeness of the oracular centers to tree cults and the common view that oak trees are somehow integral to them is also evident in a story that Temple mentions. In certain myths, Athena, the patroness of Athens, placed an oak timber from the holy sanctuary at Dodona, in the hull of the *Argo*, the mythic boat sailed by the hero Jason.[6] Because of this, the *Argo* could speak to Jason and his sailors, the Argonauts, and guide them at crucial moments during their journeys.[7] The ark of Utnapishtim (a god with a fishlike armor cascading from his fish mouth-like crown) carried fifty great gods called the Anunnaki, offspring of one of the earliest mother goddesses, An. The implication is that the wood from which the boats were made somehow transmitted information to the heroes.

The mythic history of the arks is relevant, as the early matriarchal symbols of trees as protection during great epics reappear in similar mythologies. In the Gilgamesh epic, each of his fifty companions (like Jason's fifty Argonauts) carried with them a specially felled tree for their journey.[8] As they are oarsmen, it is tempting to think that the trees were simply oars. However, the symbolism might easily be much deeper; Temple believes that this is almost certainly the case, and that they might have believed in a mystical connection with their homeland through the native trees they carried. There was a very close relationship in Greek mythic thought between trees and the water, as water in general and the sea specifically was considered feminine and the domain of the goddess.

Prehistoric Cretan Tree Matriarchies and Oracular Centers

The iconography of most early cultures, including those in the Mediterranean basin, naturally includes trees and plants as primary images, and these are almost always associated with goddesses. In the early history of the bounteous island of Crete, the land was covered with huge forests, although it is almost barren today. The fertility of the land was celebrated by worship of the goddess, who provided abundant wood for houses, spears, and ships, as well as foodstuffs like almonds, pears, and other fruits.

Goodison postulates that the various plants used by the people of Crete each had its own deity, as well as its own symbolism and worship rituals. Often each Cretan subculture or region had its own fertility goddesses, who carried boughs and wore bird headdresses, and are also shown as trees growing out of rocks or symbolic hills of stone. These fertility goddesses are also often depicted with bare breasts, indicating their fertility and ability to nurture, and with snakes in both outstretched hands, showing the healing energies they wielded as a result. Like most fertility cults based on the natural planting year, the various stages of the crops are represented in the iconography found on seals and carvings. What is fascinating is that in such imagery it is the bough or the tree that is in the center, with human figures grouped around it, rather than the other way around—vegetation is of primary importance. This is very different than our more modern view of nature, where humans are central and nature peripheral.

A fascinating byway of research into early Cretan symbolism is that the double-headed axe, although assumed by (predominately male) scholars to be a symbol of a supreme male deity or thunder god such as Zeus, is almost never seen in the hands of those deities. Rather, it is commonly shown wielded by goddesses, particularly fertility goddesses associated with tree worship. Indeed, the symbolic axe was used to cut trees down in a sacramental way. This, and sometimes also the ritual sacrifice of an animal, was a woman's task in Greek and especially Cretan societies. This act had to do with veneration with fertility, the underworld, cycles of birth and death and rebirth, and resurrection, all common themes of matriarchal tree goddesses throughout the world.[9]

8

~~~

THE CHRISTIAN STORY OF THE
PARADISE TREES OF EDEN

Even Paradise itself . . . was but a kind of . . . sacred grove,
planted by God himself, and given to man
—THE FOLK-LORE OF PLANTS

WE KNOW FROM GENESIS 2:9 that the Tree of Knowledge of Good and Evil and the Tree of Life both stood at the center of the Garden of Eden. There is an obvious polarity between the two trees in Eden, one representing sin, and the other, redemption. After being told not to eat fruit from the tree of good and evil, Eve succumbed, bringing consciousness into the world. After what was considered the temptation of Eve, Adam and Eve were sent away from Eden. God not only turned them away, but prevented their access to the Tree of Life forever. Ever afterwards, these seminal acts were considered in Judeo-Christian religions to be what is called the "original sin." We have been lead to believe that by being born human we have committed a cardinal

Raphael, *Adam and Eve* (ceiling panel), Palazzi Pontifici, Vatican, between 1509 and 1511

Carving at Notre Dame showing Adam, Eve, and the Serpent

sin and must therefore spend our lives atoning.

Schama acutely observes that the entire Biblical story is accompanied by references and symbols of trees. He cites "the timber history of Christ—born in a wooden stable, mother married to a carpenter, crowned with thorns, and crucified on the Cross."[1] He also mentions a powerful twelfth-century story about Adam being brought a seed from one of the trees from Eden, which he puts in his mouth, where it sprouts into the sacred history. The story Schama recounts culminates in Jesus Christ's crucifixion, which is often shown being enacted on a tree rather than a cross. Schama mentions a series of biblical episodes with the images of trees transforming from dry and barren states into ones that sprout into life. These stories harken back to the early vegetation myths of rebirth and resurrection. This motif was imported wholesale into the New Testament and remains there today.

The symbolic parallel between a barren tree and a fruitful tree abounds. The traditional tarot card of the Hermit often shows the Hermit standing between a barren and a fruitful tree, representing a choice between fruitful and barren ways of seeing our journey through life. This image appears in many medieval illuminated manuscripts known as Books of Hours that depict the calendar years, as well as in many Christian religious paintings.

An interesting quirk of this symbolism in Christianity is inherent in the traditional methods of illustrating the serpent that tempts Eve, wrapped around the Tree of Knowledge of Good and Evil. In *The Fall*, a scene by Michelangelo in the Sistine Chapel, the serpent is shown personified as a woman with a serpent's body, clearly expressing the association between tree, serpent, and woman. Michelangelo's scene also makes it very clear that the Tree of Knowledge of Good and Evil is deeply connected to the feminine on a visceral as well as symbolic level. The clear implication is that the feminine was the agent of temptation in Eden and remains so.

Michelangelo, *Expulsion from the Garden of Eden*, Ceiling of the Sistine Chapel, Vatican, 1508–1512

If the Tree of Life signifies eternal life or immortality, then by listening to the serpent and partaking of the apple from the Tree of Good and Evil, Adam and Eve lost the gift of immortality. However, the snake has an ancient and venerable history as an extremely positive symbol of the feminine, sexuality, and healing energies. But as Laurence Gardner mentions, for many centuries in Christianity the snake has been a negative symbol of lost paradise, of evil and temptation.[2]

The hooded cobra represented feminine power and knowledge in matrilineal Egypt, and this symbol always surmounted the headdresses of the pharaohs. Asklepios (also called Aesculapius or Asclepius), the medicine and healing god of the Greeks who brought medicinal arts to humanity, utilized snakes as a primary element of the center dedicated to him at Epidaurus, on the Peloponnesian peninsula. Since Asklepios was the mentor and teacher of Hippocrates, his symbol of entwined snakes then became the emblem of the healing profession, seen in the emblems of both the American Medical Association and British Medical Association. All doctors take the Hippocratic Oath, derived from those times. The symbol of the snake entwining a staff was in turn derived from ancient Sumerian images of a serpent coiled around a staff, which was a symbol of the royal lineage of kingship. What is telling in the biblical account of the expulsion of Adam and Eve is that the serpent was in fact the guardian of sacred knowledge. This makes one think that perhaps the patriarchal god didn't want Adam and Eve to have this valuable knowledge; he went so far as to threaten them with death for eating the apple. Gardner believes that Eve decided to take the sacred knowledge on her own, and that the One God was angered.[3]

The Roman Church has continually concerned itself with the minutiae of scripture to debate exactly which wood (oak, ash, yew, or holly, among others) was used for the cross upon which Jesus Christ was crucified. A similar argument exists as to the lineage, variety, and particulars of the piece of the thorn bush from which the crown of thorns was made. The thorn was reputedly brought to England with the Holy Grail by Joseph of Arimathea as the Glastonbury Thorn, an ancestor of which still grows in the shadow of the now-destroyed cathedral at Glastonbury.

There is a telling quote about the spin used to transform pagan sacred sites to those of the Christian church by the seventh century Pope Gregory. Gregory justified the actions of the proselytizers of his time, who were converting these sites on a regular basis. He said, "When these people (the pagans) see that their shrines are not destroyed, they will be able to banish error from their hearts and be more ready to come to the place they are familiar with, but now recognizing and worshipping the true God."[4] We now know that this is a quite powerful statement in many ways, as the church has followed the practice of many religions by using the sacred places known to pagan cultures as vehicles for their own ends. In the process, they tried as best they could to eliminate or lessen the original meaning of the sites and their inherent symbols. In my book *Sacred Landscapes* I explore this motif at length, as many of the most sacred places on the face of our earth have been appropriated by the patriarchal religious.[5]

Frazer's books mention that Roman festivals involved a conversion of the manic goddess Cybele into a pine tree. Her ceremonies afterward involved sending people into the woods to fell and carry sacred pine trees back into Rome. They also simulated the blood of the original martyr in order to represent the resurrection of nature, which happened to coincide with the Christian celebration of Easter around the Spring Equinox.[6]

Schama mentions other stories in which the cutting down of formerly sacred trees actually created changes in belief among rural pagans. For example, a Christian saint once tried to fell a giant oak sacred to Wotan (the German equivalent of Jupiter or Zeus). When it fell into the glade and miraculously split into four huge parts, this was seen as an example of Wotan's divine intervention. Of course, ultimately the wood from the tree was made into a wooden oratory dedicated to St. Peter. As Schama sarcastically notes, this isn't the only shameless hijacking of pagan values related to trees and forest glades that was committed by the Church in medieval times.[7]

What is extraordinary about this process is that the Church has condoned the wholesale destruction not only of cultures that are still embedded in the natural world, but also of the natural world itself. The Church has, in many cases, attempted to obliterate the pagan undercurrent of belief that has been around for millennia, and might even be more prominent today than it has been for hundreds of years.

Traces of the early vegetation and tree cults remain all over the medieval churches and cathedrals in Europe. Chartres Cathedral, located west of Paris, is a great example. It was built on top of a much older Druidic temple, which was in turn built on an underground spring that was a matriarchal temple to the goddess. The famous Black Madonna or Virgin of the Crypt remains in a dark chamber directly underneath the altar in the cathedral's sanctuary above. The crypt and its Black Virgin are still objects of veneration to the many pagans throughout Europe and is a startling reminder that the Church never really eliminated such obvious traces of the earlier goddess beliefs.

Vegetation symbols abound in the cathedral wherever one looks: in the carving, in the tombs' form and symbols, and of course in the stained glass. Schama mentions the representations of Bacchus (a Roman god similar to Pan or Dionysus), and Druidic oak twigs, leaves, and acorns, all of which can be found in the cathedral's rose windows and on the South Portal. They may decorate a Catholic cathedral, but they are also obvious symbols of rebirth and resurrection.[8] The Green Men (decorative features showing faces covered in leaves, related to pre-Christian vegetative deities) grace cathedrals and churches throughout Europe, particularly in England, where they often lie at the crossings at the apex of the church in an abstract form that requires close observation to identify properly.

Closer to our time, the movie *Avatar* premiered to amazing ticket sales and reviews by the establishment—and a thorough condemnation by the Catholic Church. *Avatar* portrays an alien planet where the object of worship is a giant sacred tree that communicates with the populace through tendrils that tap into spiritual energies. This communication extends to all animals and living beings in the ecosphere. The idea of such power is still considered a threat to the Church. After the launch of the movie and its accompanying positive reviews, the Vatican newspaper and radio station called the film emotionally unengaging, and said that it tries to replace divinity with nature.[9] Official Vatican Radio said the movie "cleverly winks at all those pseudo-doctrines that turn ecology into the religion of the millennium," adding, "Nature is no longer a creation to defend, but a divinity to worship."[10]

This may just seem like a reactionary response to a movie that isn't all that sophisticated. However, the Pope himself responded in a way that betrays much about the ongoing attitude of the Church toward reverence for the natural world. In a World Day of Peace message, "the pontiff warned against any notions that equate human beings with other living things in the name of a 'supposedly egalitarian vision.' He said such notions 'open the way to a new pantheism tinged with neo-paganism, which would see the source of man's salvation in nature alone, understood in purely naturalistic terms.'" This is quite predictable, coming from the head of the church that perpetuates a two-thousand-year-old patriarchal belief structure. He then explained that "while many experience tranquility and peace when coming into contact with nature, a correct relationship between man and the environment should not lead to 'absolutizing nature' or 'considering it more important than the human person.'"[11]

This is truly extraordinary, as the Pope's statement implies that humanity is not an integral part of nature, but somehow higher or beyond its ken. In a time when we should be working to create a new and more spiritual ecological vision that shows our interdependence with nature, this is a potentially dangerous idea. We must realize that human intervention has a measurable impact upon the natural world, and that (as studies have shown) if we don't change our habits of consumption, we could easily bankrupt our natural resources in the foreseeable future.

John of Patmos' Book of Revelation, the last book of the New Testament, describes The New Jerusalem, a city in a golden age in the future after the apocalypse. In 21:1–2, he describes the new heaven and the new earth and places the premier redemptive symbol of the tree of life in the center:

And I saw a new heaven and a new earth: for the first heaven and the first were passed away; and there was no more sea.

And I John saw the holy city, new Jerusalem, coming down, from God out of heaven, prepared as a bridge adorned for her husband.

He is very specific in his description of this Christian paradise, including the fact that it is a cosmic temple resonating with planetary rhythms. John Michell's *City of Revelation* describes this fascinating imagery and analyzes its geometries. Saint John goes on to say,

In the midst of the street of it, and on either side of the river, was there the tree of life, which bare twelve manner of fruits, and yielded her fruit every month: and the leaves of the tree were for the healing of the nations.[12]

What intrigued Michell is the symmetry of the Bible, as it begins with Adam and Eve and the Tree of Knowledge, and it ends with the Spirit, the Bride, and the Tree of Life.[13]

9

The Acacia Goddess

Monotheism begins with a god who hates trees.
—John Lash, *Not In His Image*

In the statues of her that survive, the Canaanite fertility goddess Ashtoreth (or Astarte) is always accompanied by her serpent. The fertility goddesses of Crete were shown as bare-breasted, with snakes wrapped around their arms. The symbolism of fertility and the mother goddesses are intimately associated with water, the sea, and the generative quality of snakes as primary symbols of the dominance of the feminine. Profound changes occurred when the goddess-worship-based, pantheistic, and matriarchal cultures that had been reverenced for millennia were overcome by the newly arising patriarchal and monotheistic religions. The focus of belief shifted from earth goddesses to sky gods to an off-planet deity, the one supreme God Jehovah. Gradually, the more modern monotheistic

Demeter and Persephone in the Eleusinian Mysteries, ca. between 440 and 430 BCE

religions were born, and the ancient gods consigned to the past as outworn pagan beliefs.

In his provocative book, *Not in His Image*, John Lash discusses the value of the earlier, earth-oriented religious beliefs that were prominent all over the world before the advent of the monotheistic religions. He writes that thousands of generations lived and worked and believed in a deep connection with the earth, sustaining the development of "vineyards, baths, aqueducts, roads, earthworks, ancient groves of olive trees and oak trees, salt marshes, stone works of all kinds including great megalithic circles such as Stonehenge and Newgrange . . . Everywhere one goes outside the urban conglomerations in modern Europe, the land has been touched and shaped by human hands, skillfully, even lovingly managed."[1]

Lash bases much of his book on the importance of Gnostic ideas from just before the advent of Christianity. The Gnostics proliferated these ideas four hundred years before they were almost completely wiped out. Among the primary documents of Gnosticism are the Nag Hammadi codices, which have challenged standard perceptions of early Christianity after being discovered in a cave in upper Egypt in 1945. What is ironic is that in ancient times, the place where they were found was called *Sheniset* in Hebrew, "the acacia of Seth," indicating that it was most probably a Gnostic sanctuary.[2] The early Christians were forcibly deterred from incorporating influences of the previous Middle Eastern Gnostic matriarchal cults, which were characterized by nature worship and a reverence for the natural world. The Gnostics' version of Christianity was more abstract and messianic. In one of the Nag Hammadi codices ("On the Origin of the World", II,5), the world is described as the creation of an off-planet lone creator god who was, as a result of being independent of a female counterpart, in denial about nature. The Gnostics' primary goal was to shift the core focus of the Abrahamic religions—those that trace their lineage back to Abraham, such as Judaism, Christianity, and Islam—which was that humanity was special, having been made in god's image rather than from the earth. This perspective naturally created a denial of nature.

The Gnostics worshipped a divine universal mother, Sophia, as the incarnation of ancient wisdom ("Sophia" is Greek for "wisdom"). To them, she was a fallen goddess embodied in the earth. The Nag Hammadi codices contain an ecological myth that resonates with the concept of Gaia, the earth, as a living system.[3] The mythos of Sophia is that she is an imaginative feminine contrast to the patriarchal totalitarian religions that advocated salvation at the expense of the environment and the earth itself. Lash mentions many examples of such earth-based religions revering nature, including the Thompson Indians of the American Northwest:

> At first Kujum-Chantu, the earth, was like a human being, a woman with a head, and arms and legs, and an enormous belly. The original humans lived on the surface of her belly. [The old legend recounts how the Old One] transformed the sky woman into the present earth. Her hair became the trees and grass; her flesh, the clay; her cones, the rocks; and her blood, the spring of water.[5]

Monotheism took a powerful stance on nature worship early in its history, and its message has changed very little since then: worship of the natural world is not only undesirable—it will not be tolerated. As Lash says, "It makes the earth devoid of divinity, its inhabitants subject to an off-planet landlord."[6] And he is a jealous landlord.

A biblical quote makes this very clear: "Ye shall utterly destroy all the places, wherein the nations which ye shall possess served their gods, upon the high mountains, and upon the hills, *and under every green tree.* And ye shall overthrow their altars, and break their pillars, and burn their groves with fire; and ye shall hew down the graven images of their gods, and destroy the names of them out of that place."[6] The entire Bible is full of situations where, in times of crisis, the Hebrew people were considered to have "regressed" to the worship of their previous gods and goddesses, such as Ba'al and Asherah, meriting the wrath of God. Because pagan deities are of the earth and therefore exist everywhere, eliminating all traces of them was a terrific task. And since most of the early goddesses were tree goddesses, the association was complete: the places where the women worshipped, in the groves of trees outside of the sacred enclosures of the men, were to be destroyed, leveled to the ground.

Lash mentions that the dominance of the jealous patriarchal god "demanded the desecration of the holy sites of nature-loving people, trees, and sacred objects in every green place."[7] This denial of the natural world was extended to include any references to the goddess, and indeed sexuality, except for procreation. The places where goddess worship continued were almost always groves of trees. Even when trees had been cut down, worshippers gathered around the stumps of trees, using them as altars and pillars representing their faith. Lash remarks that the Canaanite fertility goddess Asherah's name *means* "sacred tree," and further states that this connection is redundant as all trees were sacred to the ancient people. In Deuteronomy 7:26 it is stated clearly, "Neither shalt thou bring an abomination [an Asherah] into thine house, lest thou be a cursed thing like it: thou shalt utterly detest it, and thou shalt utterly abhor it; for it is a cursed thing." Jehovah is here warning the Israelites not to erect an Asherah near his altar.

In the Bible the Hebrew word "Asherah" is mentioned many times in a variety of contexts. It can refer to the goddess or her worship, and can even extend to the idols or statues representing her. It also refers to groves of trees under which the women worshipped the goddess. Asherah is often shown as a woman becoming a tree, or vice versa, and we can still see images of this miraculous transformation in seventeenth-century alchemical texts. It is also speculative but possible that one of the twelve tribes of Israel, Asher, was a comingling of Israelites and Canaanites descended from Asher himself as a surrogate of Asherah.

Since Judaism does not permit images of Jehovah, by necessity the primary religious symbols are abstract, such as the seven-branched candlestick called the menorah, which is an ancient symbol of Judaism known to be at least three thousand years old. There is also the nine-branched menorah used on Hanukkah, which is the festival closest to the Winter Solstice, falling anywhere from late November to late December because of the lunar calendar used in Judaism. As the menorah is an abstraction of Asherah, it remains as a symbol of the goddess of the sacred trees. So we see that the very representation of the suppressed feminine goddess cults absorbed by Judaism is revered as a symbol that has eliminated most of its naturalism and connection with the trees from which it was first derived. This parallels the demotion of Asherah, who went from the consort of Ba'al and later Yahweh, to being literally written out of the Bible.

Among the Hebrew names for God were Yahweh and Adonai (meaning "lord" or "father" or "Our Lord"), and he was originally paired conjugally with his consorts, Anath and Asherah. This sexual partnership is apparent in Proverbs, where God is paired from the beginning with his feminine complement, Hochmah, or Wisdom. Proverbs 3:8 compares wisdom itself to a tree: "She is a tree of life to them that lay hold upon her: and happy is every one that retaineth her." However, at some point the qualities of the goddess symbolized by the tree, who created the material world, are taken over by the jealous male god Yahweh. She is further denigrated as being responsible for the fall from grace when she and Adam are expelled from Eden.

The challenge of Asherah remains throughout the Bible. Solomon was the sacred king who built his temple in Jerusalem, but he was also disdained for allowing his many wives to build sanctuaries (asherah) to their deities around Jerusalem. According to 1 Kings 11:8: "The temple of Jerusalem was simultaneously dedicated to Yahweh and to the Queen of Heaven. The pillars Joachim and Boaz were said to stand for the sun and moon. Before it stood the Asherah." This shows that the sacred tree was an integrated symbol at this earlier time of Jewish history. This continued until Solomon's son brought the golden calves of the ancient worship into the temple itself. The Queen of Heaven was a powerful deity, and it took many generations to change this fact. In spite of the pressure to turn away from old, goddess-worshiping beliefs, the Israelites continued to revere her and kept an awareness of her power alive. There is a Christian parallel in the Virgin Mary, who has, in many cases, become more important than Jesus Christ. At various times the virgin cults have been far more powerful, going so far as to endanger the patriarchal papal rule that has existed for almost two thousand years.

Manasseh (a king of Judah in the seventh century BCE) allowed altars for Ba'al and made a grove of Asherah, as did other kings of

Israel, until the balance shifted and such tolerance became a thing of the past. A "hidden text" was found that restored the worship to Yahweh only, and this led for the first time to true monotheism. Ultimately the Old Testament was rewritten to exclude references to these earlier sins, including the great influence of the Queen of Heaven and Asherah. This is described in Exodus 34:13 as follows: "But ye shall destroy their altars, break their images, and cut down their groves: For thou shalt worship no other god: for the Lord, whose name is Jealous, is a jealous God."

ACACIA AND ASHERAH MYSTERIES

As we have already seen, the Bible makes it clear that Noah used acacia, or *shittim* wood, to build his ark. Jacob planted *shittim* trees in the Land of Goshen for his descendants because they would be needed in the future during the exodus. After exodus, God commanded that this wood was to be used in making the temple of Solomon itself, as well as the temple's furniture and the sacred Ark of the Covenant, which contained the tables of the law that Moses brought down from Mt. Sinai. The *shittim* wood was also used to make the budded staff of Aaron, which is another fertility symbol, obviously from the earlier cults. A gold pot of manna was also constructed. In the same way, the ark was made from this wood, overlaid outside and inside with gold, and surmounted with two winged cherubim with their wings folded in toward each other. These are the only carved or graven images permitted in Judaism. It is also common to make the spine of the torah, the sacred books of the Bible, out of acacia wood. This is a fascinating bit of symbolism, because many of the most powerful relics of Jewish history are made out of this wood, sacred to the goddess Asherah.

Acacia wood is also central to the myth of the Egyptian founder deities, Isis and Osiris. When Osiris was entombed and then drowned after being murdered by his brother Set, it was a green acacia tree that grew up from his coffin, due to the magic created by Isis and Nepthys. Since Osiris was the god of the underworld and resurrection, he falls into the category of the gods crucified on wood, trees, or in his case, entombed in a wooden coffin.

It is not surprising that the worship of acacia would survive even if it had to mutate into different forms, as this wood was integral to many of the mystery cults in the early Middle East. Its influence continues as a primary symbol in Freemasonry and Masonic lore. Manley Palmer Hall asserts that initiates of the higher mysteries often carried either the thorn branches or flowers of acacia in their hands to symbolize this sanctified ritual process.

Acacia is also integral to the mysteries of Freemasonry in that the early Masons were aware of its deeper secret symbolism. They understood that it was emblematic of the immortal soul. This was especially evident in Freemasonry's ritual murder of the architect of the universe, Hiram Abiff. Although the act took place on desolate ground, an acacia tree sprouted on the very sport of his burial, identifying it. In the Masonic funeral service, for which Mozart wrote his famous music, it is said: "This evergreen is an emblem of our faith in the immortality of the soul. By this we are reminded that we have an immortal part within us, which shall survive the grave, and which shall never, never, never die." This ritual is ancient in practice, as the Greeks were known to place acacia wreaths at the head of graves. It is also thought that the ancients substituted acacia for other plants because they thought it

Freemason document

incorruptible, thus symbolizing the incorruptible nature of the soul, as well as signifying the initiation process.

In the funeral service, the Master Mason says, "My name is Acacia," and this means: "I have been in the grave, I have triumphed over it by rising from the dead, and being regenerated in the process, I have a claim to life everlasting." And so acacia is associated with eternal life and the mystery of resurrection.

Acacia as a Sacrament

It is not surprising that acacia is considered by some to be a sacrament that gives experiential access to the goddess, given its influence on spiritual tradition beginning in ancient Sumeria. This was the case regarding the myth of Persephone and Demeter, which was the foundation of fertility cults that were fundamental to the Eleusinian Mysteries. The culture surrounding these ceremonies lasted almost a thousand years. In this myth, Demeter's beautiful daughter Persephone symbolizes the fertility of the yearly cycle. She is abducted by the god of the underworld, Hades (or Pluto, in the Roman variant of this story). Her mother makes an arrangement with Hades that would allow her daughter to return to the world above ground from spring until winter, when she is required to return to her husband. While Persephone is above ground crops and nature grow and flourish, but when she returns to the realm of the dead, nature similarly became dormant.

We know that the Eleusinian mystery cults incorporated materials such as sheaves of barley, wheat, corn, pomegranates (symbolizing fertility, death, and resurrection), and poppies (an opiate) in their rituals. It has been suggested that these plants could have produced mind-altering substances that were used in the worship of these secret rites. Wheat is known to harbor a hallucinogenic fungus that could have produced the sensations of death and rebirth that initiates were thought to have experienced first-hand. There have also been many suggestions that these mysteries used the barley fungus ergot as a sacrament. Gordon Wasson, an ethnomycologist and scholar of the historical uses and sociological impact of fungi, believes that hallucinogens were a significant part of initiation rituals in ancient

Greece, Crete, and in Mesoamerica, and might even have been a component of the Indian magical substance soma.[8]

Acacia is quite magical as a tree because it possesses a number of sacred qualities that are not commonly known, and that resonate quite astoundingly with the symbolism we have discussed. Acacia roots and bark are known to have hallucinogenic qualities due to the high concentration of the substance DMT (Dimethyltryptamine), which is a naturally synthesized chemical used in ayahuasca rituals by shamans in the Amazon delta. It also exists in minute quantities in our body, and it is speculated that it triggers transcendental experiences when ingested. The experience of acacia, when taken with a tea made from *Peganum harmala* (Syrian rue), a neuro-uptake inhibitor, is to be instantly transported into the realm of the goddess of fertility, into a brilliantly colored and mysterious world of pure feminine life. Having experienced this on a number of occasions, the author can say that it evokes an extremely brief but enlightening experience in which one is transported into the realm of a very powerful feminine fertility presence, what we call the Acacia Goddess. It is fascinating because the sources that tell of the predominant use of acacia in the early Middle East, in early Semitic and Jewish cultures, in Egypt, or in the Masonic mysteries never mention or infer this other use. The mystery is that this substance is also unique in producing an experience that is consensual, in that everyone partaking goes at the same time to exactly the same inner, sacred place. This in itself constitutes a great mystery.

THE YGGDRASIL WORLD ASH TREE

The ash Yggdrasil suffers anguish,
More than men can know:
The stag bites above; on the side it rots;
And the dragon gnaws from beneath.
—POETIC EDDA, QUOTED IN ROBERT GRAVES, *The White Goddess*

LEGENDS OF THE WORLD TREE abound in many cultures, but one of the most fantastic and powerful is that of the Yggdrasil ash tree of the Norse myths. Its branches arch out into the sky and its gigantic roots dig deep into the darkest realms of hell, as it symbolizes the integration of heaven and earth. It was both a mythic place and representation of the entire created universe. For the Norse culture, which worshipped the tree as the universal temple, *temple* and *tree* were interchangeable words, as they were in Celtic languages.

Friedrich Wilhelm Heine, *Ash Yggdrasil*, 1886

The Yggdrasil is a symbol of Life, Time, and Destiny, and rises up from a great void in space called Ginnungagap, which has a form very much like an egg. The shaft of its trunk is the axis of the world, around which heaven itself revolves. The three roots of the tree reach into realms that symbolize aspects of reality in the world. The spiritual world is based in Asgård, the home of the Åesir, the gods. Asgård also contains Valhalla, the realm of fallen warriors and heroes, which is watered by the fountain Urdar. There are many divisions of Asgård, such as the Well of Fate Uroarbrunnr, where the three female Norns, prophetic old crones, weave the destinies of all beings to determine their fates and also water Yggdrasil to keep it alive. The Norns are similar to the triple goddesses of ancient European myth and they carve the destiny of all humans onto the tree itself, in a runic language.

There are also other godly realms within the Yggdrasil tree, such as the land of the Vanir, the minor gods, and Aflheim, the realm of the elves. These evocative names are reminiscent of the place names J. R. R. Tolkien uses in *The Lord of the Rings*, as Norse was one of the main influences on Tolkien's writing. The terrestrial root of the World Tree is in the abode of men, called Midgård. This realm is watered by Mimir's (*Mimir* means "memory") well of wisdom under the roots of the tree. This is the well to which Odin (also called Wōden or Wotan) was required to give an eye in order to be able to see beyond the material world and into the spiritual worlds. Odin lost an eye in exchange for gaining the capacity to prophesy the future, and, at his own request, gained spiritual sight by being crucified on the world tree without sustenance for a period of days. As a result, this well of mystical water contains stories, visions, and memories. This tale is a catalyst for the vision quests at the core of the beliefs of the Scandinavian shamans and warriors.

Hel is the realm of the dead, and contains the dwarves' forges, built into the mountains. It is watered by a spring called Hvergelmir. These three root worlds support the middle earth realm of Midgård, separated from the space around it by sheer cliffs of rock and ice. A huge Midgård snake biting its tail enwraps these worlds, enclosing a circular sea that surrounds the entire world. In the middle of the land is a gigantic mountain, and on the top of the mountain is the city of the gods. Only by traveling across the Rainbow Bridge called Bifrost can gods and men connect.

In the topmost branches of the tree, under the North Star, are various mythic animals that symbolize the "senses" of the gods, and are subject to the great god Odin. Other inhabitants of the top of the tree include an eagle—mounting the apex of the tree, which presides over all beings—and the hawk between the eyes of the eagle, which sees everything that happens in the worldly realms. At the base of the tree's roots is entwined the serpent Nidhung, who slithers into the abyss, and gnaws at the roots of the divine tree. When he succeeds, the tree dies and the rule of the god will end, leaving humanity vulnerable to a godless world.

Befitting the Scandinavian warrior and Viking ethic, the Norse worldview is powerful and highly dependent upon fate. Their gods are

....

NECKLACE AND RINGS

THE FATHER GOD GAVE ME,

FOR MY VISIONS

AND PROPHECIES.

FAR I SEE AND WIDE,

THROUGH ALL OF THE WORLDS.

—Poetic Edda

similarly destined to live through vast world ages, punctuated by mass destructions called Ragnarök (the final destiny), when the gods lose power and favor, and the world must be recreated anew.

These evocative images of the world tree seem fanciful to us, but they are among the most visual and poetic expressions of early humanity's need to make tangible the connection between earth and heaven. The tree is possibly the most powerful metaphor expressed in ancient mythologies in this regard. Nature, fertility, creation, sexuality, wisdom, knowledge, and many other profound qualities of humanity are described in relation to the tree. Rain comes through holes in the fabric of the world tree. If one climbs high enough, one can ascend to heaven. The various regions of the tree's growth symbolize places where men and their souls exist. It is as though the universe was seen as a giant tree-house wherein humanity, the angels, the gods, and devils all live, their domains determined by the various levels that they inhabit. However, all are connected as a vast, eternal living organism. Their tree is a vast, eternal living organism that symbolizes the universe.

ODIN THE GOD OF PROPHECY

The myth of Odin reinforces much earlier stories about crucified gods, who symbolize and enact the yearly death of the world of nature. All are crucified on trees or some equivalent as a seminal initiation. Odin shares qualities similar to the Greek Hermes or the Egyptian Thoth, as he is a psychopomp, or "guide of souls."

As Ralph Metzner mentions: the Egyptian god of vegetation Osiris was trapped in a wooden chest and then absorbed into a tree; the Greek god who brought fire (and consciousness) to humanity was chained to a rock; Christ was crucified on a wooden cross; the Sumerian fertility goddess Innana was imprisoned within an underground vault; and he

W. G. Collingwood, *Odin's Self-sacrifice*, 1908

even includes a reference to the Hanged Man of the traditional tarot deck, who depicts these many crucified gods and goddesses.[1] In addition, the Hindu god Krishna was impaled on a tree; Mithras, the god of the Persians and the Roman centurions, was crucified on a tree and rose from the dead, and is often seen as a prototype of Christ; and the Aztec god Quetzalcoatl was similarly crucified and reborn.

All of these gods voluntarily allow their self-sacrifice to nature as a way to bring wisdom and knowledge of the spiritual domain to the world of men and women, and this sacrifice is almost always enacted on a World Tree. It is not accidental that all these great prophetic and mythic beings were initiated on the tree of life, the tree of prophecy, as it is the way by which they ascend to heaven. As comic shamans, this is a fitting way for them to make their way to the higher and exalted realms of the deities. Even today, certain Native American tribes such as the Sioux conduct a sun dance ceremony that involves the participant being hooked to a tree in the bright sun without food or water for long periods of time.

Odin is the god of prophecy and discovered the runic tree language, and the story of his ritual ordeal is part of the Elder Edda, the "Sayings of the High One." In this, Odin hangs from the Yggdrasil, the world ash tree itself, where he gains perfect sight into the many realms of the spirit. Odin's ability to overcome death is a central motif of his journey on the tree. In this way, Odin is a prototype of shamanist activity, of being an intermediary between the worlds.

In his many writings, Joseph Campbell describes Odin as being both dead and alive at the same time, and therefore representing, on behalf of

....

I KNOW THAT I HUNG

ON THAT WIND-SWEPT TREE,

THROUGH NINE LONG NIGHTS,

PIERCED BY THE SPEAR, TO ODIN SACRIFICED,

MYSELF TO MY SELF,

ON THAT GREAT TREE

WHOSE ROOTS

NO ONE KNOWS.

—Ralph Metzner, *The Well of Remembrance*

Ludwig Burger, *The Norns Urðr, Verðandi, and Skuld Under the World Oak Yggdrasil*, 1882

all humanity, an expression of our many hopes and fears about death and life. The tree is a perfect vehicle for this ambiguous mystery, in that so much of its associated lore involves both males and females. In Adam and Eve's expulsion from Eden, the tree expressed the same duality in Eden, in the form of the Tree of Life and the Tree of Good and Evil.[2]

The tree is portrayed in these Norse myths, but it is also associated in one creation myth with the first humans, because the word for ash is "Askr," which is also the name of the first pair of humans. By this association, we can see them as tree-beings brought into consciousness by Odin and his kin.[3] This world ash is also very tall, green much of the time, and is very powerful in many realms. This leads Metzner to speculate that rather than the ash tree, the tree at the center of so many Norse myths might have been a yew, because yew trees have many substances in their wood and berries that also have hallucinogenic qualities. The yew was used by Nordic peoples in shamanistic rituals as a guide and catalyst for their journeying. The World Tree is an axis that penetrates the nine worlds, which are aspects of existence and the pathways between these various elements of consciousness. These nine worlds are traveled by the shamans in their quests for knowledge

....

I WEEN THAT I HUNG ON THE WINDY TREE,
HUNG THERE FOR NIGHTS FULL NINE;
WITH THE SPEAR I WAS WOUNDED, AND OFFERED I WAS
TO ODIN, MYSELF TO MYSELF,
ON THAT TREE THAT NONE MAY EVER KNOW
WHAT ROOT BENEATH IT RUNS.

—Poetic Edda

and the essence of spirit. In his book, Metzner shows a Nordic "Tree of Life" or "Tree of the Worlds," which I reproduce here. We can easily see that such diagrams of world trees, world axes, and trees of life, are prototypes of both the diagrams of family trees and also the Kabbalistic Tree of Life.

THE WHITE GODDESS AND THE CELTIC TREE CALENDAR

Beloved, gaze in thine own heart,
The holy tree is growing there;
From joy the holy branches start,
And all the trembling flowers they bear.
The changing colors of its fruit
Have dowered the stars with merry light;
The surety of its hidden root
Has planted quiet in the night.
—WILLIAM BUTLER YEATS, "THE TWO TREES" (1893)

THE ENGLISH POET ROBERT GRAVES wrote his treatise *The White Goddess* (1948) as "a grammar of poetic myth," a rediscovery of the Celtic tree calendar and its rich and profound symbolism. He determined to investigate the myths associated with the Celts' runic language and poetry, as well as their calendar. These deeply emotional

Ogham stone, Kilmalkedar, Ireland

and paradoxical legends and their poetic manifestation throughout English and Celtic cultures fascinated him. In the Prose Edda, Odin and his sons Vili and Ve take trees and create men from them: Odin gives them humanity, life, and mind; Vili gives them movement and intelligence; and Ve gives them their senses.

While it is known that Robert Graves took poetic license in his book, his message is clear: the Celtic cultures revered trees, and trees were as much an integral part of their intellectual landscape as their physical world. Graves mentions that what he calls the "Beth-Luis-Nion" (Birch-Rowan-Ash) tree-alphabet was "a relic of Druidism orally transmitted down the centuries."[1] In this alphabet, "beech" is a synonym for "literature," since writing tablets were made of this wood, and the word has an etymological correspondence with the ancient Germanic word for *book*.[1] Since the runic alphabet was composed of branches, this makes sense. When we see trees, we are seeing ancient ways of communicating with their nature spirits.

In addition to lending their shapes to the letters of the runic alphabet, trees possessed magical powers, because the alphabet itself was considered magical. The Celts associated different trees with corresponding

....

THE MOTHER OF OUR SONGS, THE MOTHER OF ALL OUR SEED, BORE US IN THE BEGINNING OF THINGS AND SO SHE IS THE MOTHER OF ALL TYPES OF MEN, THE MOTHER OF ALL NATIONS. SHE IS THE MOTHER OF THUNDER, THE MOTHER OF THE STREAMS, THE MOTHER OF TREES AND OF ALL THINGS. SHE ALONE IS THE MOTHER OF THE FIRE AND THE SUN AND THE MILKY WAY.

—Universal Mother myth of the Kagaba people of Colombia[2]

mythic heroes, or gods and goddesses. Each tree had roles to play in myths and legends, and many also were healing plants in Celtic lore.

The tree alphabet has thirteen consonants and five vowels, and Graves correlates the thirteen consonants with the thirteen lunar months of twenty-eight days each that compose a solar year (13 x 28 = 364), a sequence that was considered "lunar" because the lunar month corresponds closely to the menstrual cycle of women (although the Anomalistic Month—following the actual elliptical orbit of the moon—is 27.55455 days). The following is the sequence of trees that compose the Celtic calendar:

B is for Beth and birch at the Winter Solstice in December. Birch is self-propagating and its twigs were used as whips; its wood was utilized for ceremonial staffs in Roman times and also throughout the Celtic world. As its time is the end (and beginning) of the year, birch staffs were used for beating out the old year.

L is for Luis and rowan, mountain ash, or quickbeam (which means "tree of life") and is the second month of the "quickening" of the year. Quickbeam was used to expel demons, for protecting houses from lightning and climactic influences, and to create magic during battles and difficult times. Red was the color associated with death in early cultures, as red ochre paint was used to mark the bodies of dead warriors in the first ancient grave burials.[3] Red rowan berries were similarly magical, as they were a food of the gods and therefore were only to be eaten at sacred meals or ceremonial occasions. Rowan was the wood of choice for making witch's magic wands and also for protection, and therefore acted as a preventive device to resist magic. Rowan thickets graced divinatory and oracular sites, where the future could be discovered through visions and dreams.

N is for Nion, ash, and the third month. Ash trees were the most sacred trees in Celtic and Roman mythologies and were associated with strength and valor in battle, and also the rebirth that was thought to be the fate of brave warriors. As we have seen, the Yggdrasil World Tree was an ash.

F is for Fearn and alder and the fourth month. Alder is a mythic battle-witch tree, best in battle, which might be an allusion to the fact that it is considered the best with which to make charcoal. It also contains resins that make its wood water resistant.

S is for Saille and willow or osier. Willow was considered to be enchanted, and its association with the goddesses—Hecate, Circe (or Hera, the wife of Zeus), and Persephone—led to its being worshipped by witches as the mistress of death and the underworld. It is a lunar tree and was used to make wicker baskets and could bind things. The willow's bark was used in many herbal remedies, perhaps because it contains salicin, a chemical from which aspirin is derived. This tree always grows near water, typical of its lunar association with the goddesses who are the watery element.

H is for Uath, whitehorn, and hawthorn. Hawthorn has a reputation for bad luck, particularly in regards to sexuality and marriage, and as a result, those wanting to conceive or give birth were encouraged to avoid hawthorn for the entire month. It is also associated with destructive elementals, and this time of the year as well as the tree itself is considered a bringer of obstacles—the destruction of a hawthorn tree signaled bad luck and great peril.[4]

D is for Duir and oak. Oak is sacred to Zeus, Hercules, and the chief of the Irish gods Dagda, as well as the Scandinavian god Thor, and other thunder gods. It is also associated with the Middle Eastern deity we have discussed, El, who might be a prototype for Allah. Oak is associated with Midsummer Eve, when the oak king is sacrificed and the midsummer fires burned oak wood. Oak roots are thought to go as far below ground as its branches go into sky, and so it is the tree associated with both heaven and hell.

T is for Tinne and holly or evergreen oak. Holly is associated with birth and fertility, and the increase of passion at the prime of the year around the summer solstice. It is also associated with Christ and the crucifix, a T-shaped cross.

C is for Coll and hazel. Hazel concentrates wisdom. Mythically, it is grouped with the sacred salmon. The fish feed on hazelnuts that fall into the rivers and streams, giving them their characteristic red spots. Salmon and hazel are both involved with the flowering of the arts as "seeds" that give life and bloom to creativity by evoking the nine muses, the number that is sacred to hazel. Hazel is knowledge of hidden wisdom and profound truths, as it was, and still is the wood of choice for dowsing rods and twigs.

M is for Muin and vine. Vines provide wine and came north into the British Isles with the Danaan people, a mythic race of Irish legends. It is a tree of exhilaration and wrath. People are warned against eating grapes because of their association with the Crown of Thorns, and the assumption that the juice of the berries was somehow like Christ's blood. Like the acacia tree, it has associations with the mysteries.

G is for Gort and ivy. In the ancient autumn nature revelries, it was traditional for participants to wrap ivy and its yellow berries around fir branches and run around the woods and fields destroying everything in their path. Ivy was sacred to the resurrected gods, including the Greek god Dionysus, and the Egyptian god of the dead, Osiris, and it was fitting that their festivals happened around the winter solstice, the darkest time and death of the solar year, just before the birth of the New Year. Ivy is sacred to Dionysus, the god of wine and intoxication. Graves mentions that many public houses in England still use ivy on their pub signs to show this ancient association with the spiral growth patterns of the vines.

NG is for Ngetal and reeds. Canna-reeds come from the thick roots that were ancient symbols of royalty; bunches of reeds were often carried by royals, and Middle Eastern prophets. Egyptian pharaohs shot arrows with reed shafts at the sun god. The Irish people used reeds for the essential task of thatching their houses.

R is for Ruis and elder. Elder trees grow beside rivers and lakes and have always been associated with witches' magic. But while birch, another wood associated with magical power, is fashioned into cribs thought to protect babies from evil spirits, elder is considered unlucky, and is therefore never used for that purpose. However, elder's flowers, berries, and inner bark are all used for natural medicines, and elderberry and elderflower wines are still available in northern Europe, even though its berries are associated with death, and particularly the crucifixion of Jesus. Some believe that the cross was made of elder wood, and it is often used as a funeral wood. Along with cypress and yew, elder is commonly planted in cemeteries. The white elderflowers are associated with the matriarchal White Goddess of the title of Graves's book.

There are also five trees that correspond to the vowels of the Beth-Luis-Nion alphabet. In the course of the year, each tree corresponded to and ruled for a period of thirteen weeks.

A is for Ailm and silver fir. Silver fir is a female tree like a yew, typically very old, with branches that overhang close to the ground. Silver fir is sacred to the moon and the goddess cults as it is the color white. This is the tree around which the vines or ivies were wrapped in spirals to celebrate Dionysian ceremonial revels. This tree is also associated with the "Queen of the Druids," the "mother" of the entire tree alphabet.[5]

O is for Onn and furze. The furze tree or gorse has thorns and golden flowers. It is associated with the sun and with springtime, when the warmth of nature begins to return. It is the first plant that bees visit to initiate the growing season.

U is for Ura and heather. Heather is sacred to the Egyptian goddess of fertility, Isis, and also to other Mediterranean love goddesses. Heather is red and hence signifies passion, and is also associated with bees, which are drawn to them. Heather is also linked to mountains, where it grows. Graves notes that in less mountainous regions, the substitute for heather is the linden tree.

E is for Easda and white poplar. White poplar is symbolic of autumn. Its leaves are white on one side and much darker on the other so that they flash in the wind. They are also divinatory because of their connection to the moon and darkness, and have an oracular history. Black poplars were thought of as funereal trees and therefore symbolized death and Mother Earth.

I is for Idho and yew. Yew trees are thought of as the death tree throughout Europe, and associated with the Greek and Roman goddess of death, Hecate. Since yew trees grow in predominately horizontal directions throughout cemeteries in Britain, it is not surprising that its myth is that the roots of these omnipresent trees grew into the mouths of all corpses buried in the church yards. Not only was yew wood used for bows and arrows in medieval times, but archers used a well-known poison derived from yew berries to make toxic arrows.

The tree alphabet permeated Celtic and Druidic culture. The runes and their associated trees corresponded to poems and Celtic heroes, as well as the to earlier gods and goddesses of the Mediterranean regions. They were associated with fingers in divinatory systems for reading hands, and informed the structure of the calendar year. On festival days, the Celtic calendar and mythic religion were so closely connected to the progress of the year that people felt similarly aligned with the natural world. Because of this connection, they were naturally responsive to natural and planetary rhythms. It is essential that we understand how these connections might still be valuable for us, as they direct us to honor trees as valuable signposts in our journey back into integration with the natural world. How many of us even have a clue about this extensive language, much less make any attempt to use it in gaining a closer identity with our own inner nature?

Druids, who were also often poets, founded their colleges in groves of trees, most often oak trees. The holiest Druid sacred places were oak groves, and one sees them still all over Wales. The word *nemeton* ("grove" or "sanctuary") is found in numerous ancient Celtic place-names, such as Nemetobriga ("exalted grove") in Spain, Drunemeton ("oak grove") in Galatic in Asia Minor, and in present-day Nymet and Nympton in Devon. Anglesey's sacred groves may also have been oak groves.[6] The Druidic poets were also called "oak seers," probably because they expressed their prophecies through this wonderful resonant poetic medium.

The following tale is fascinating as an example of such Celtic lore. The story is about the enchantress Cerridwen, whose children were a beautiful girl and an ugly boy. She decided to compensate for this imbalance by imbuing her boy with magical wisdom and intelligence.

Cerridwen created a cauldron of inspiration that she brewed for a year of seasons, into which she put magical herbs gathered in the right planetary hours. However, a local boy spilled some liquid from the cauldron onto himself by mistake, and, licking it off his finger, instantly knew everything: past, present, and future.

As he ran away, the boy found that, due to the power magic of the potion, he was able to avoid Cerridwen's pursuit by changing into a succession of animals. When he changed shape, she did also, until she finally caught him, but only after they had both gone through almost endless transformations. She swallowed him and subsequently gave birth to him as her own child, Gwion. In horror, but also out of respect for his physical beauty, she put him in a bag, which she then threw into the sea. He later washed onto the shore, only to be found by a prince who had been fishing. The prince came to love the child as a son and named him Taliesin, who came to express extraordinary wisdom and was known as a great bard.[9] His best poetry were riddles, and Taliesin and the bards used trees as context for the magical states of Welsh lore. Thus trees were an evocative medium for this entire culture's mythology and magic. As an interesting sidenote, the renowned American architect Frank Lloyd Wright, who was of Welsh extraction, called both his houses in Wisconsin (and his school in Arizona) Taliesin, out of respect for this Druidic hero.

~~~~~~~~~~

12

MESOAMERICAN AND NATIVE AMERICAN TREES

I am trying to save the knowledge that the forest and this planet are alive,
to give it back to you who have lost the understanding.
—PAIAKAN, CONTEMPORARY KAYAPÓ INDIAN LEADER[1]

A THOUSAND YEARS BEFORE THE CHRISTIAN era, the Mesoamerican Olmec culture flourished in south-central Mexico. It is well known that the Olmecs and later Mesoamerican civilizations had a sophisticated agricultural society and an astronomical system that helped them orient their buildings very precisely. Magnificent pyramids belonging to these cultures dotted the jungle landscape. Many were oriented toward the Pole Star, the Big Dipper (which points to the Pole Star), the Pleiades, and the rising and setting points of the zodiacal ecliptic, or the rising or setting positions of the sun and other planets.

Mayan world tree, Izapa stele

It is becoming increasingly accepted that the Mesoamerican civilizations were also aware, at a very early time period, not only of the Milky Way galaxy in which our sun is located, but the exact center of the galaxy, hundreds of years before this was known in Western cultures.

The calendar was particularly prominent in Mayan culture, which flourished from c. 250–900 CE. The Mayan creation epic, the Popul Vuh, was an oral myth of the Quinché Maya of Guatemala, first recorded in hieroglyphics .[1] The Popul Vuh is quite astonishing because it demonstrates that the Mayans were aware of astronomical cycles such as the procession of the equinoxes. Their texts define this phenomenon by the use of the word "wobble" to describe the earth's north-south axis moving backwards relative to the zodiac in a grand cycle of about 26,000 years. This is significant because it shows an understanding of the workings of the earth, sun, solar system, and Milky Way galaxy superior to any knowledge Western society possessed at the time.

What is most interesting from our viewpoint is that the Mayans' mythology, culture, and astronomy were all integrated into a type of tree religion. Anthropologists know that there were many animals and plants to which the Maya attributed magical powers, and were given a place in their integrated cosmology, and trees were quite central to this. Mayan kings were also shamans, who were in touch with the nature spirits of animals and plants. They considered the plane of human existence to be sacred. In the Mayan conception of the world, the human domain floated in a cosmic sea and, as in ancient China, it was often pictured as being the back of a huge cosmic turtle split into four cardinal directions. Each compass point had its own tutelary tree, bird, color, gods, rituals, and prayers.[2] The Mayans' highest deity was associated with the center of the world, which to them was commensurate with the origin of the world. At the mystical and important center, called the Wacah Chan ("six sky" or "raised-up sky"), was the Sacred Tree—the world axis, linking all directions and all of the upper and lower realms together. Much like the Yggdrasil tree, its branches soared into the heavens of the Otherworld, just as its roots penetrated deeply into the watery Underworld, and its trunk was in the Middleworld. The tree functioned both as a link between the various realms of existence and also as the passageway between them. This act of communication was symbolized by two serpents, the Vision Serpent and also the Double-headed Serpent Bar.[3] Once again, the World Tree and the snake or serpent represent a dependent relationship, however here the symbology has an astronomical significance as well. The connection between the astronomical cycles of the world and the World Tree is powerful indeed, and tells us much about the prominence of the Sacred Tree as a paramount status in world myth and cosmology in many cultures.

Linda Schele, an expert on the Maya, mentions in her book *The Forest of Kings* (1990) that the Mayan image of the cosmos was like a circular map with the World Tree at the center, and with its influences radiating toward the periphery. She describes their cosmos in living terms:

> Along the upper edge of the image arches the living sky, the Cosmic Monster, which contains within its body the great ancestral Sun and Venus. The rains, its holy blood, flow in great scroll from the mouth of its crocodilian head and from the stingray spine on the Quadripartite Monster as the opposite end. The World Tree, *Wacah Chan*, emerges from the head of the god Chac-Xib-Xhac (the Eveningstar) as he rises from the black waters of the portal. The trunk of the World Tree splits

Ceiba tree in front of the Great Jaguar temple, Guatemala

to become the Vision Serpent, whose gullet is the path taken by the ancestral dead and the gods of the Otherworld when they commune with the king as the forces of nature and destiny.[4]

The Maya brought the power of otherworldly beings into their culture through their notorious sacrifices. These were enacted in the plazas of their grand cities, ringed with pyramids. Their plazas featured stone slabs called "tree-stones" with images of Mayan sacred kings. These tree-stones symbolized the surrounding tropical forests. Since the pyramids were symbolic mountains, the doors entered symbolic cave entrances, within the caves, ritual ceremonies were held on special days. From one such mythical royal mountain, the World Tree was said to grow out of a cave door, marking and signifying the place as the center of the world; it was in the form of a *ceiba*, a huge tropical tree that naturally grows out of caves high up in mountains in this region. Therefore the plazas replicated many of the significant features of the surrounding natural world: forests, trees, animals, mountains, and caves. The repetition of rituals enacted in such sacred places for hundreds of years instilled them with sacred energies. By performing these ceremonies, the Maya ensured that the sacred places were under the protection of the entire pantheon of gods and retained access to the gods' energies forever.

As a specialist in Mayan cosmology, John Major Jenkins summarizes in his 1998 book, *Maya Cosmogenesis 2012*, that because it is known that the inhabitants of the Americas originally migrated from Asia over the land bridge that used to exist between Russia and Alaska, it would be logical that a belief system similar to the Mayans' existed earlier in Asia. He quotes evidence that the orientation of the

Emperor of China's residence in the Hidden City in Beijing was also oriented toward the Pole Star.

Belief systems incorporating a world axis are found throughout the world. These similar beliefs are widely associated with entryways to the underworld, which the Maya called the "Dark Rift," a kind of royal road that leads to the underworld, which is called royal because it is the place of creation and origin.

The complex worldview embodied in Mayan culture is important for us to understand. Their four-directional Sacred Tree, also identified as a calabash or ceiba tree, is a symbolic and mythic intersection of heaven and earth, and is also a representation of the intersection of the plane of the Milky Way galaxy and the plane of the ecliptic, the path along which the sun, moon, and planets move through their cycles. Their profound cosmology was centered on this astronomical feature, and they were able to locate it in the night sky.[5] This shows that the power of the Sacred Tree is one that goes far beyond a symbol or myth. It is no less than our orientation within our galaxy.

NATIVE AMERICAN CREATION MYTHS

Native American cultures respected trees because they were integral to their creation myths and stories. Many Native Americans believed that the first humans emerged from a chaotic underworld, a place of unformed beings and objects. The Ancoma Pueblo myths say that the first humans were sisters. Because they grew up in such darkness, they could not see each other, but only touch each other. Grandmother Spider fed them, and gave them a basket of seeds and images of all the animals they would bring into the world. Trees sprouted from the seeds the sisters planted, but they grew very slowly because of the darkness. Eventually one of the trees penetrated the ground, and found the light above. This allowed the sisters to emerge into the light world above and create all of the species that lived there. They also placed mountains at the cardinal directions. Ultimately one of the sisters gave birth to the Pueblo people.[6]

Another Pueblo creation story is a variant of the first one, where nature helps the Pueblo people emerge into the world.

> Twin brothers dwelling in the dark underworld wondered if there was any light up above. First, Cottonwood went up but could not see any sunlight. Then the cedar tried, but came back down. Then the spruce tree was going to try. But Spruce saw that he would need an opening. . . . So Woodpecker Boy flew up to the top of the spruce tree and began to peck at the ceiling. . . . Eagle flew up to the top of Spruce tree and built a nest for Badger. . . . As Badger worked upward, Spruce grew taller, so Badger could more easily carry out this task of helping the people to reach the upper world inhabited by the Sun. The people thanked Spruce and told him that his branches would forever be used in Pueblo prayers.[7]

What is noticeable in the Native American creation myths is that there is a profound interconnection between nature and humanity, and that the natural world and the world of humans are codependent at every level; often the intermediary that originally establishes and then maintains this interconnection is trees. Trees link the higher and lower worlds, acting as a conduit that allows communication between the formlessness of the lower worlds and the intelligence of the upper world. Trees are essential vehicles for universal integration. Native American myth is often indicative, in this way, of a belief that the world is delicately balanced, sensitive to any alterations that we might impose upon it. We must stay in touch with the tree spirits in order to learn to integrate the multiple worlds in which we live.

One Native American creation myth starts with a time before earth and life existed. During this time, it was said of the Woman Who Dreamed: "One night she dreamed about a tree covered with white blossoms, a tree that brightened up the sky when its flowers opened, but that brought terrible darkness when they closed again." Trees figure in all the important Native American creation stories. The wise men and women meet under their sacred council trees for ceremonies, in order to sanctify them.

The Koyukon Native Americans understand that everything—including air, landforms, sky, and weather—has spiritual power. Also all elements, plants, and animals are interconnected, and all such beings and elements' function is to monitor the progress of the human being. In the Koyukon cosmos, all species are attuned to the behavior of the beings around them. As genetics professor David Suzuki and science writer Peter Knudtson state in *Wisdom of the Elders* (1993):

> For example, if a person displays disrespect toward a birch tree by casually casting aside wood shavings while making snowshoes, the spirit of the tree can retaliate. When the person next searches for a piece of wood, the spirits may hide themselves, making it more difficult for the person to find them.[8]

This mutual observation of species is inherent in the Koyukon's worldview and enshrined in their mythology. The Koyukon believe that all life forms have their own life strategies and behaviors, and also, in a particularly profound idea: "like all life-forms, each plant *was transformed from a human* near the end of the primordial Distant Time era."[9] After the last deluge, during a much earlier time of creation called the Distant Time, Raven spirit was like Noah, saving pairs of all species. All humans morphed into botanical beings, so the plant world is in reality transmigrated humanity. This ensures a high degree of respect and indeed brings another whole dimension to plant-human communication.

The plants are harsh judges of humans, probably for good reason. They pass judgments and mete out punishments to humans who abuse the plant world. All of the magical plants and animals that are part of daily lives in the Koyukon world are powerful beings imbued with sacred qualities—a spiritual residue of the Distant Time.

As discussed in Valliant's book about the northern spruce trees, the Koyukon Native Americans place an extremely high value on these magnificent tree spirits, which they call *biyeega hoolanh*.[10] They rate the strength of this particular tree spirit with their highest and most important animal totems, the result of the tribe's intense reliance upon these huge trees, which grow to a height of a hundred feet or more. Apparently the Koyukon language is itself a testament to the high value placed on the trees; as Suzuki and Knudtson note, they have "at least forty terms for describing parts of trees and kinds of wood, terms used mainly or exclusively for this species."[11] Their shaman healers use spruce heads to remove illnesses, both physical and spiritual. Many tribespeople bond with the trees as spiritual allies on their hunting journeys.

They also revere silver or paper birch trees, those trees that stand out so beautifully in northern forests. The tree's bark peels have the most amazing fragrances, and are used to make baskets and other implements, as well as canoes. As this tree is so important for the tribe, severe limitations are placed on how many of them can be used and how they are to be utilized. The Koyukon therefore harvest the bark in warm months in such a way that the tree can protect itself in the frigid winters. The Koyukon way of life is characterized by reverence for their surroundings and of all species of living beings, and is therefore in almost total harmony with nature.

An anthropologist of the Koyukon discovered their belief that even after a tree has been slain or harvested, it retains an emotional energy and spirit. Even after it dies, all of the tree's chips, branches, leaves, and other elements retain this sacred quality. The various trees native to their region all carry myths rationalizing their appearance and accounting for the essence of their healing and other spiritual energies. In one tale, the primordial mink-man approached a group of human-plant figures called tree-women, to tell them of the death of their husband Raven, the transformer spirit of the sacred Distant Time. Each of the tree-women communicated their feelings for the deceased Raven by wounding their bodies in unique ways, and this is why the patterns and colors of the bark of trees are so different. Each tree carries the sadness in its own unique way. For example, the alder-woman pinched herself until she bled, so the Koyukon use her tree coloring as a dye.

FOREST MAGIC

The Kayapó Indians of the Xingú River in central Brazil have traditionally occupied themselves by reforesting the savannah in almost invisible ways. These ingenious people create small islands of trees, like portable forests or islands of forests in the wilderness, in such ways that it reinvigorates the entire complex ecosystem in which they live.

At the beginning of the rainy season, the Kayapó Indians create small islands of forests that mimic the growth patterns of the jungle around them. They create natural mulch, and plant in such a way that the small island then begins to grow and reproduce without any intervention at all. The trees are then used for the various things the villagers seek in the wild, including foodstuffs, material for buildings and utensils, and medical products for their healing rituals. These island forests serve as a natural environment for animals and cover for the tribesmen.

The Dayak Indians of Sarawak, Borneo, in Southeast Asia, live in a mountainous, dense jungle crisscrossed by many rivers, and their culture is unique in that its worship of trees and cosmology are both highly developed. Above all, they respect and cherish wild bee honey from the very highest trees in the forest, which is harvested in a coming-of-age ceremony for young men. The ceremony entails climbing up into the trees via their massive trunks and ascending to the treetops in treacherous conditions, alone. To the villagers, this recalls the mythic journey of their hero, Aki Ungkok, who climbed so high that he found himself in an upside-down world above, the home of the Grandfather of the Moon and of the Seven Stars, who were Dayak creator gods. Just as the mythic hero discovered the secrets of agriculture from the beehive, so the young initiate finds the honey at the top of the trees. As he harvests it, he sings the honey song that recounts all of the other young men who have taken the journey before him. As Suzuki and Knudtson remark in *Wisdom of the Elders*, "Native knowledge of this primary ecological interdependency among plants, animals, and humans, along with a sense of their ancient and shared creation stories, must contribute to the widespread Native belief that the botanical realm, or at least some portion of it, is permeated by the sacred."[12]

The Yoruba people of Nigeria have a sophisticated creation mythology with a plethora of gods and their spirits.[13] In their most important myth, the great sky god Olodumare observed from heaven that the world was no more than a vast ocean. He gave his two sons, Obatala and Oduduwa, a bag, a hen, and a chameleon, and sent them down to the ocean. He lowered a great palm tree onto the surface of the waters so that the brothers landed in the tree's branches. Obatala hacked at the bark of the tree and made a strong palm wine from its sweet sap, became drunk, and fell asleep. Oduduwa opened his bag, and sprinkled the sand that he found inside onto the water's surface. Then he released the chameleon onto the sand, which moved ahead very cautiously, and behold, the land held firm. Oduduwa also found some dark earth in his bag, which he scattered on top of the sand. When he put the hen on it, it began scratching and pecking, flinging earth far and wide, and where it landed it formed the great continent of Africa.

Among the ancient Hawaiian natives, the underworld was accessed through a tree near a cleft in the earth after death. Joseph Campbell relates such a tale, where the entrance to the other world is signaled by a deceptive and magical tree with two sides: one that is green, lush, and fresh, and another side that is dry and brittle.[14] Contrary to logic, the soul must climb up and down the tree through the dry branches without touching the green ones, which would send him down to annihilation. This view makes a point that the world is defined by such paradoxes as life and death, light and darkness, and that the tree embodies them as is its nature. An individual's ability to understand and learn to negotiate the mysteries of the tree of life and death is derived from the merits he has earned during his life. Due to the decisions he has made, he might be reborn as one of a variety of animals that are guardians of the living. Assignation of a particular animal is determined according to an individual's rank.

It is clear from these creation mythologies that trees are a potent and useful symbol, made manifest in the actual trees that surrounded early humans. It would seem to be obvious that trees are a universal link between the heavenly sky and the earth.

13

⁓

TREES AND OUR
ECOLOGICAL FUTURE

*In Greece beautiful woods of pine, oak, and other trees still linger on the slopes
of the high Arcadian mountains, still adorn with their verdure the deep gorge
through which the Ladon hurries to join the sacred Alpheus, and were still,
down to a few years ago, mirrored in the dark blue waters of the lonely lake of
Pheneus; but they are mere fragments of the forests which clothed great tracts
in antiquity, and which at a more remote epoch may have spanned the Greek
peninsula from sea to sea.*
—SIR JAMES FRAZER, *THE GOLDEN BOUGH*
"THE WORSHIP OF NATURE" (1926)

TREES ARE THE LUNGS OF our planet, serving as major converters
of carbon dioxide into the oxygen that we breathe. But we have
honored them by clear-cutting millions of acres of trees all over the
world, particularly in the Amazon rain forest, the forests of the Pacific
Northwest, across the North American continent, and in Europe. It

Amanjiwo palm tree overlooking Borobudur

is essential that we restore the sanctity and sacredness of trees so that humanity will stop eradicating one of the most important sources of our well-being. Only by conjoining the sacred with the ecological agenda of our age can we turn this unfortunate and dangerous abuse of the natural world of Gaia into a healthy planet Earth.

In *The Golden Spruce*, Vaillant remarks that forests seem like positive places of serenity and peace, while in fact the reality of old-growth timber forests is really the opposite. In Vaillant's estimation, forests are "ruthlessly competitive places," where the fight for light dominates all life. Light is integral to the process of manufacturing oxygen through photosynthesis. The giant trees of old-growth forests are profound and complex organic machines that perform this necessary process in continual competition with other forms of life there. As Vaillant notes, the forest floor abounds with tiny organisms; however, the great trees are really like veils of living material on a scaffold of molds, fungi, and inorganic material, and the main photosynthetic processes take place behind the protective bark layer in a very thin membrane. The tree is continuously bringing up massive amounts of water from the depth of its roots through the capillaries behind the bark hundreds of feet into the air, only to release it into the atmosphere, where it becomes rain that feeds the roots of plants again.

The Golden Spruce traces the history and significance of ancient myths and legends about trees from our distant past to the present. We support this vision, which shows the gradual transition between the earliest cultures, many of which seem to have been matriarchal, if not matrilineal like ancient Egypt, and to a certain extent, Judaism. We have traced these religions' gradual transition to a more patriarchal position on the natural world. The modern scientific paradigm takes this tendency further, from humanity being immersed in nature, to distancing our existences from nature, to being completely divorced from it except as an abstract idea. In our world, unfortunately, nature and the earth are seen by many as simply a source for raw materials to be exploited in whatever ways possible. Prominent important issues such as global warming are denied most vehemently by those whose beliefs systems render nature in the most abstract terms.

In *The Golden Spruce*, Vaillant is not advocating a return to nature, nor a return to the idea of the "noble savage" and a scrapping of civilization. However it is essential that we begin to make a more powerful effort to communicate with nature, to learn from the natural world, and to encourage young people to go back to the woods, to climb the trees, and discover the language that awaits them there.

The Ringing Cedars series of books describes a phenomenon that is powerful because it advocates a vision of the natural world that has tangible and positive manifestations. Its visions of nature are very real ones, to the extent that these books exhibit a truly new paradigm showing us how to relearn nature's language—before it is too late.

The central character, a woman called Anastasia, lives in Siberia in a kind of communion with the world of nature. As a result, she can teach us about new approaches that could restore our belief in the inherent goodness of the world and its people. She also presents real ways to get back in touch. She sees that:

> The peoples of the earth have so many words with different meanings. There are so many diverse languages and dialects. And yet there is one language for all. One language for all Divine callings. It is woven together from the rustlings of the leaves, the songs of the birds, and

the roar of the waves. The divine language has fragrance and color. Through this language God responds to each one's requests, and gives a prayerful response to prayer.[1]

Anastasia can feel and understand this language, but what about us? She asks:

> How can it be that we have let it go unheeded for centuries? Cold logic dictates that if God created the Earth and the Nature that lives all around us, then every blade of grass, every tree and cloud, the water and the stars can only be His materialized thoughts. But we simply pay no attention to them, we trample them, break them, disfigure them, all the while talking about our faith. What kind of faith is that? Who are we really worshipping?[2]

The movie *Avatar* made an impact because it presents an "alien" world called Pandora, with a population living totally in tune with nature. The natural world depicted in the film is fantastical and beautiful, but also profound. The Na'vis' primary deity is a tree called Eywa, and all inhabitants of the world have a visceral, physical, and energetic connection through the spirit of Eywa. In an article in the British *Globe and Mail*, the filmmaker Richard Meech talks about the parallels between the vivid and enticing world of *Avatar* and the visions that many have reported, and even painted, after taking the ceremonial and shamanic Amazonian substance ayahuasca. This sacred hallucinogenic concoction, and many others like it, are derived from vines and trees, and all over the world many Westerners and other non-natives are realizing that these substances hold a key to recreating the communication with nature.

Meech interviewed many people who have tried ayahuasca and discovered that their experiences were very similar to the Na'vis' engagement with the natural world portrayed in *Avatar*. This connection is one that everyone in the society experiences directly; there is a neural network available to all, and a process of "an egoless merging with one's surroundings, coupled with feelings of love for all creation."[3] While this film has provoked strong reactions from the Vatican, from the military establishment, and other either right-wing or fundamentalist Christian organizations, it "begins with plants, the most humble of nature's creations—but also the most powerful, for life cannot exist without them."[4]

Trees are such a critical part of the natural balance of things that we must learn to hear their language, and to respect their countless values, and to realize that we cannot replace them. Trees were on earth before us, and most likely will be here after we are gone. However we use them or understand them, trees are in our lives to stay, and in our hearts in so many ways. Since I have been researching and writing this book, virtually everyone I have talked with has told me a story about their early love of trees, how at certain points in their lives trees became symbols of solidity and trust to them. Let us not forget the immense worth of trees and do everything we can to keep them alive, and especially to pass on their myths, stories, and legends to youngsters who need to know them. Let us return to the Sacred Language of Trees.

ENDNOTES

CHAPTER I

[1] Graves, Robert, *The White Goddess*, (London: Faber and Faber, 1971), 40.

[2] Schama, Simon, *Landscape & Memory* (New York: Vintage, 1996), 14-5.

[3] Lethaby, W. R., *Architecture, Mysticism, and Myth* (New York: Dover, 2004), 35.

Louv, Richard, *Last Child in the Woods: Saving Our Children from Nature-Deficit Disorder.* http://www.grist.org/article/louv

[4] Porteous, Alexander. *Forest Folklore, Mythology and Romance.* (Chicago: American Journal of Sociology, 1928), 30.

[5] Kallir, Alfred, *Sign and Design, The Psychogenetic Source of the Alphabet*, James Clarke & Co, London, 1961.

[6] Ibid, 289.

[7] Ibid, 291.

[8] Ibid, 291.

[9] Ibid, 292.

Kapok tree with roots like snakes, Palm Beach, Florida

[10] Buhner, Stephen Harrod, *The Secret Language of Plants, Bear &*
Company, Rochester, VT, 2004, p. 160.

[11] Many television programs seek to find successive explanations of
nature.

[12] Thoreau, Henry David, poem from In the Maine Woods.

CHAPTER 2

[1] Vaillant, John, *The Golden Spruce,* (New York: Norton, 2006), 24.

[2] Ibid.

[3] Ibid, 9.

[4] Ibid, 11.

[5] Ibid, 54.

[6] See the valuable book, *The Big Burn: Teddy Roosevelt and the Fire*
That Saved America, by Timothy Egan, Houghton Mifflin, New
York, 2009.

[7] Ibid, 57.

[8] Ibid, 59.

[9] Thoreau, *In the Maine Woods,* (New York: Penguin, 1988).

[10] Ibid, 96-7.

[11] Ibid, 107.

CHAPTER 3

[1] Sinha, Raghuvir, *Religion and Culture of North-Eastern India (India:*
Abhinav Productions, 2004), 30-1.

[2] See Santillana and von Dechend's *Hamlet's Mill,* which develops
this idea of the divine millstone.

[3] Precession of the equinoxes is an astronomical phenomenon
whereby the Spring Equinox (Spring) point moves backward

through the twelve zodiac signs in about 26,000 years, creating about 2000 years old sign eras, like the present Age of Aquarius.

4   See my *Sacred Architecture* for more information about the divine tent pole and axis of the world in the development of world architecture.

5   Hall, Manly Palmer, *The Secret Teachings of All Ages (New York: Tarcher, 2003), 94.*

6   *Jung, Carl, Alchemical Studies (London: Routledge & Kegan, 1967), 197.*

7   *Ibid, 137.*

8   Jung, Carl, Modern Man in Search of a Soul (New York: Harcourt, 1955), 129.

9   Ibid, 125.

10 Jung, Carl, *Alchemical Studies*, 193-5.

11 Metzner, Ralph, *The Well of Remembrance (Boston: Shambhala, 2001), 222.*

12 Ibid, 222.

13 Jung, 195.

14 Ibid, 196.

15 Ibid, 196. Jung says that this is a direct quote from the Theatrum chemicum, IV, which is a famous alchemical manuscript dated from 1659.

16 Jung, 302.

17 Ibid, 309.

18 Ibid, 317.

19 Ibid, 318.

20 Hall, 94.

CHAPTER 4

1. Porteous, 196-7.

2. Ibid, 31.

3. Prasad-Rao, Manju, "Sacred Trees and Plants" (unpublished paper)

4. Ibid, 1.

5. Paramananda, Sami, *Upanishads* (New York: Signet, 2002), commentary.

6. Sinha, 32–33.

7. Ibid., 38.

8. Ibid., 41.

9. Ibid., 43.

10. Prasad-Rao, 2.

11. Sinha, 44.

12. Ibid., 46.

13. In the words of Nagarjuna from Khandro.net, 1998.

14. From the description of a Robert Beer painting of the Green Tara. http://www.khandro.net/deities_Tara1.htm

15. Ibid, p. 272.

CHAPTER 5

1. Eliade, Mircea, *The Myth of the Eternal Return (Princeton: Princeton UP, 2005), 125.*

2. Mackenzie, Donald, *Egyptian Myth and Legend (New York: Bell, 1978), xxii-xxiii.*

3. Ibid., 89–92.

4. Ibid., 97.

5. See my book *Sacred Architecture* for many examples.

6 De Lubicz, R. A. Schwaller, *Sacred Science (Vermont: Inner Traditions, 1982), 146.*

CHAPTER 6

1 Reik, Theodor, *Pagan Rites in Judaism (New York: Farrar, Straus, and Company, 1964), 66–68.*

2 Campbell, Joseph, *The Masks of God*, 149.

3 de Santillana, Giorgio, and Hertha von Dechend, *Hamlet's Mill*, 447–9.

4 Ibid., 469.

5 Text in parens should be New York: Schocken, 1972

CHAPTER 7

1 Eisler, Riane Tennenhaus, *Sacred Pleasure (San Francisco: HarperOne, 1996), 87.*

2 *Temple, Robert, The Sirius Mystery (Vermont: Destiny Books, Inner Traditions, 1998), 148-9. Temple also references Graves' The Greek Myths.*

3 Ibid., 150.

4 Megre, Valdimir, Anstasia: The Ringing Cedars, Part I (Nevada: Ringing Cedars Press, 2008), 53.

5 Temple, 157.

6 Temple mentions that the name Argo is interchangeable with the word Omphalos (= navel) and also connected with the sacred Hindu seed syllable Om, on 130–1.

7 Temple, 72.

8 Temple, 99.

[9] Goodison, Lucy, Moving Heaven and Earth (London: Women's Press, 1990), 112.

CHAPTER 8

[1] Schama, 219.

[2] Gardner, Laurence, Genesis of the Grail Kings (London: Bantam, 1999), 92.

[3] Ibid., 94.

[4] Schama, 216,

[5] Mann. A. T., *Sacred Landscapes* (Sterling: New York, 2010)

[6] Ibid., 217.

[7] Ibid, 219.

[8] Ibid, p. 218.

[9] Itzkoff, Dave, "Vatican Pans 'Avatar'" *New York Times*, January 13, 2010.

[10] Ibid.

[11] Ibid.

[12] Michell, John, City of Revelation (New York: Ballantine, 1977), 63-5.

[13] Ibid., 146.

CHAPTER 9

[1] Ibid., 27.

[2] Ibid., 10.

[3] Ibid., 11.

[4] Ibid., p. 178.

[5] Ibid., 227.

6 Deut 12:2–3. Quoted in John Lash's *Not In His Image* (White River, Junction, Vermont: Chelsea Green, 2006), 227.

7 Lash, 329.

8 Wasson, R. Gordon, Stella Kramrisch, Jonathan Ott, and Carl Ruck, *Persephone's Quest* (Yale: New Haven, CT, 1986). and Wasson, R. Gordon, Albert Hoffmann, and Carl Ruck, *The Road to Eleusis* (Hermes Press: Los Angeles, 1998).

CHAPTER 10

1 Campbell, 120.

2 Metzner, 220–1.

3 Ibid., 197.

CHAPTER 11

1 Graves, *The White Goddess*, 165.

2 Ibid., 38.

3 Ibid., 168.

4 Ibid., 176.

5 Ibid., 191.

6 Littleton, 254.

CHAPTER 12

1 In parens: Rochester, Vermont: Bear & Company, 2008

2 Schele, Linda and Freidel, David, A Forest of Kings (New York: William Morrow, 1990), 66-7.

3 Ibid., 68–69

4 Ibid, 70.

5   See the books that Jenkins mentions by the Maya scholar Linda Schele, *A Forest of Kings* (with David Freidel) and *The Code of Kings* (with Peter Matthews). Both books describe the highly sophisticated Mayan civilization and its cosmology.

6   After the title: (New York: Bantam, 1992)

7   Ibid., 33. There are many of these stories in Suzuki and Knudtson's book, showing the proliferation of myths of creation.

8   Ibid., 134.

9   Ibid., 131.

10 Ibid., 132–3.

11 Paiakan, quoted in Julian Burger, *The Gaia Atlas of the First Peoples* (London: Anchor Books, 1990), 32.

12 Suzuki and Knudtson, 138.

13 Ibid, 145–147.

14 Littleton, 626.

15 Campbell, 119–20.

CHAPTER 13

1   In parens: Stateline, Nevada: Ringing Cedars Press, 2008

2   Ibid, 160.

3   Meech, Richard, "Sacred brews, secret muse," *Globe and Mail*, January 29, 2010.

4   Ibid.

BIBLIOGRAPHY

Altman, Nathaniel. *Sacred Trees*. New York: Sterling Publishing, 2000.

Buhner, Stephen Harrod. *The Lost Language of Plants*. Vermont: Chelsea Green, 2002.

Buhner, Stephen Harrod, *The Secret Teachings of Plants*. Vermont: Bear & Co., 2004.

Burckhardt, Titus. *Sacred Art East and West*, trans. Lord Northbourne. London: Perennial Books, 1967.

Burland, Cottie. *North American Indian Mythology*. London: Chancellor Press, Reed International, 1996.

Campbell, Joseph. *The Masks of God*. New York: Viking Press, 1969.

Carroll, Maureen. *Earthly Paradises*. London: British Museum, 2003.

Catty, Suzanne. *Hydrosols*. Rochester, NY: Healing Arts Press, 2001.

De Lubicz, R. A. Schwaller. *Sacred Science*, trans. Andre and Goldian VandenBroeck. New York: Inner Traditions, 1982.

Eisler, Riane. *The Chalice and the Blade*. San Francisco: HarperSanFrancisco, 1987.

Eliade, Mircea. *The Myth of the Eternal Return*. Princeton, NJ: Bollingen Series XLVI, 1974.

Fabricius, Johannes. *Alchemy*. Copenhagen: Rosenkilde and Bagger, 1976.

Gardner, Laurence. *Genesis of the Grail Kings*. London: Bantam, 1999.

Goodison, Lucy. *Moving Heaven and Earth*. London: Women's Press, 1990

Graves, Robert. *The White Goddess*. London: Faber and Faber, 1961.

Gupta, Shakti M. *Plant Myths and Tradition in India*. New Delhi: Munshiram Manoharlal, 1991.

Hall, Manley Palmer. *The Secret Teachings of All Ages*. Los Angeles: Philosophical Research Society, 1968.

Higgins, Godfrey. *Anacalypsis*. 2 vols. New York: Macy-Masius, 1927.

Ingalls, Daniel H. H., trans. *Sanskrit Poetry*. Cambridge, MA: Harvard UP, 1969.

Jenkins, John Major. *Maya Cosmogenesis 2012*. Santa Fe: Bear & Co, 1998.

Jung, Carl G. *Alchemical Studies*. London: CW13, Routledge & Kegan, 1967.

—. *Modern Man in Search of a Soul*. Boston: Harcourt Harvest, 1955.

Lash, John Lamb. *Not In His Image*. White River Junction, VT: Chelsea Green, 2006.

Lethaby, William. *Architecture, Mysticism, and Myth*. London: Architectural Press, 1974.

Lewington, Anna and Parker, Edward. *Ancient Trees*. London: Collins & Brown, 1999.

Littleton, Scott, ed. *Mythology*. San Diego: Thunder Bay Press, 2002.

Mackenzie, Donald. *Egyptian Myth and Legend*. London: Gresham, 1907.

Mann, A.T., *Sacred Architecture*. Shaftesbury, UK: Element, 1993.

———, with photographs by Lynn Davis. *Sacred Landscapes*. New York: Sterling, 2010.

———, with Jane Lyle. *Sacred Sexuality*. Shaftesbury, UK: Element, 1995.

Megre, Vladimir. *Anastasia: The Ringing Cedars I*. Henderson, NV: Ringing Cedars Press, 2008.

Metzner, Ralph. *The Well of Remembrance*. London: Shambhala, 1994.

Paterson, Jacqueline Memory. *Tree Wisdom*. San Francisco: Thorsons, 1996.

Philpott, J. H. *The Sacred Tree or the Tree in Religion and Myth*. New York: Macmillan, 1897.

Porphyry. *On the Cave of the Nymphs*, trans. Thomas Taylor. Grand Rapids, MI: Phanes Press, 1991.

Porteous, Alexander. *Forest Folklore, Mythology and Romance*. Chicago: American Journal of Sociology, 1928.

Paramananda , Swami, trans. and commentary. *The Upanishads*. Boston: *The Message of the East* magazine, Vedanta Center of Boston, 1913.

Prasad-Rao, Manju. *Sacred Trees and Plants*. Private paper, undated.

Santillana, Giorgio de and Von Dechend, Hertha. *Hamlet's Mill*. Boston: Godine, 1977.

Schama, Simon. *Landscape & Memory*. London: HarperCollins, 1995.

Schele, Linda and Freidel, David. *A Forest of Kings*. New York: William Morrow, 1990.

Schele, Linda and Matthews, Peter. *The Code of Kings*. New York: Touchstone, 1998.

Sharashkin, Leonid. *The Secrets of Cedar Products*. Kahului, HI: Moving Books, 2008.

Sinha, Binod Chandra. *Tree Worship in Ancient India*. New Delhi: Books Today, 1979.

Suzuki, David and Knudson, Peter. *Wisdom of the Elders*. New York: Bantam, 1992.

Temple, Robert K. G. *The Sirius Mystery*. London: Sidgwick & Jackson, 1976.

Thoreau, Henry David. *In the Maine Woods*. New York: Penguin, 1988.

Titmus, Christopher. *The Green Buddha*. Totnes, UK: Insight Books, 1995.

Vaillant, John. *The Golden Spruce*. New York, W. W. Norton, 2005.

Wasson, R. Gordon; Kramrisch, Stella; Ott, Jonathan; and Ruck, Carl. *Persephone's Quest*. New Haven: Yale UP, 1986.

Wasson. R. Gordon; Hoffmann, Albert; and Ruck, Carl. *The Road to Eleusis*. Los Angeles: Hermes Press, 1998.

Zimmer, Heinrich. *Myths and Symbols in Indian Art and Civilization*, ed. Joseph Campbell. Washington, DC: Bollingen Series VII, Pantheon Books, 1966.

INDEX

PICTURE CREDITS